WHEREVER HE LEADS

Cora Ney Hardy in a Hausa Tribe woman's dress

WHEREVER HE LEADS

BY CORA NEY HARDY

HARMONY HOUSE PUBLISHERS
LOUISVILLE

First published in the U.S. in 1999
Harmony House Publishers Louisville
P.O. Box 90
Prospect, Kentucky 40059
502-228-2010
Copyright ©1999 by Roy L. Jones

All rights reserved. No part of this book may be used
or reproduced in any manner whatsoever without
written permission, except in the case of brief
quotations embodied in articles and reviews.

Library of Congress Number 99-71638
International Standard Book Index Number 1-56469-055-5

First American edition
This book was printed on acid-free paper
Printed in Canada

DEDICATION

Dedicated to the Educational System of the State of Kentucky which, although often maligned and seldom receiving the acclamation it deserves, continues to produce outstanding teachers and educators.

CONTENTS

Foreword ix

Introduction xi

In the Beginning 4

Surprise! Surprise! Surprise! 13

The "BUSH"! 18

And Down it Came! 30

To Scared to Speak 35

The Christmas Tree 37

Seidei 39

Discipline 49

'Twas the Day! 56

Dr. Jombo 66

"Casing the Joint" 75

Memorable Meals 79

Stressful Change 91

The Two R's: R&R 95

The Three R's; Reading 'Riting and 'Rithmetic 103

A Desperate Journey 109

Furlough 113

Biography 128

FOREWORD

The contents found within these covers were not created to be a book. They were a series of notes, recalled by the author from her own experiences, for the purpose of a Doctorate Degree Dissertation. After her death, they were discovered on audio tapes where, being blind for the last eight years of her life, she had spoken them. Through the work and assistance of several of her contemporaries, they have been pieced together to make a story. During the compilation every effort was made to ascertain the factuality of the names, places, dates and events. Due to the absence of the actual author during this process, if an error exists, it is truly unintentional.

What kind of a story is it? Simply put, it is a 'love story'. About the actual experiences of a very special woman who loved God and His church, her country and native state, her family and friends, children and her teaching profession and all peoples of all races, creeds and religions.

It is more than that. It is also a story about a woman from the veritable sod of the heartland of America. A spot that is neither north nor south, nor east or west, but from its actual heart, who shared her love and skills with the children of two completely diverse continents.

Miss Hardy at the time of her Foreign Mission Board appointment.

INTRODUCTION

If Cora Ney Hardy was not a Renaissance Woman she was certainly a Transition Woman having lived and worked on more than one side of a variety of arenas of change and development during her lifetime. How to illuminate in the most meaningful way the fascinating facets of a life well-lived and contributions significantly made? As near-neighbors and next-door-neighbors and fellow-laborers through more than a score of years and close friends for still another score we can only suggest a framework to provide the reader with helpful insights by which to interpret the contents of this work. Otherwise, there is too much life, too many accomplishments to cover.

Cora Ney was truly an international figure with one foot firmly planted in her beloved Kentucky Bluegrass and the other in the tropical soil of Nigeria. She could pivot freely between the two without losing her balance. She never substituted one for the other but skillfully used the two to complement each other. Her biological family in the United States and her mission family were both supremely important to her and she could relate to both and help them relate to one another in such a way that they became a blended whole. Those who knew her chiefly in her Nigerian context always felt we were cousins—another branch of the family—to her American relatives. Evidently, they felt the same.

Another important collection of worlds in which she operated smoothly and freely was political Nigeria. Her years there bridged the span from closing colonial days of the British Empire to the dawning decades of independence under a new Nigerian flag. She had little difficulty moving from the formality of colonial ritualism to the more pragmatic era of nation-building. She was equally at home on the dais in hat

— INTRODUCTION —

and gloves or in the kitchen, garden, or building site where the perspiration flowed. She could confer and plan with dignitaries in their offices and then hammer out the application in the classroom.

Nigeria's educational system presented additional need and opportunity for flexible transition. Cora Ney stretched hands in both directions to pull, literally, educational opportunities for girls from a limited, almost non-existent status, into a position where girls could rival boys in capability and accomplishment. Nigeria was no less a man's world when she left than when she got there. Nevertheless, while maintaining every bit of her femininity, she took her place among the men and helped pave a smoother road of leadership for both-missionary and Nigerian women. Furthermore, she calmly and sometimes painfully bridged the troubled waters while expatriate leadership and administration gave way to indigenous ambition and responsibility.

Not the least of her transitional skills manifested themselves as she moved between the tried and successful methods of the past and the innovative, creative experiments of the future. Cora Ney was invariably willing to try something new, knowing that it would require much more work and a lot of 'fine-tuning' before hoped-for results could even be faintly detected. Her usual response when so confronted was "Well, at least let's give it a try!" And with that she was already out the door to make a plan and give it a try. Who got the credit was never a problem. More than once she did most of the work while receiving little or no acknowledgement for the job well done. In fact, she seemed to prefer the attention and praise go to someone else who might have done less but-in her thinking-needed the credit more.

Nor was she hesitant to expose the operation of her strong but simple Christian faith to the scrutiny of persons of other faiths and cultures. Not only was she sustained and strengthened by her faith, she earned esteem for herself and her belief system while demonstrating her love for others and respect for their faith. Many times, the regard she gained was instrumental in another's transition to new faith.

The romantic in all of us is appealed to by that transition when Cora Ney became Mrs. Roy Jones. It's the stuff of which novels and movies are made when an accomplished, successful, fulfilled professional woman—the maiden missionary on the brink of retirement, having lived 30 years less than 10 degrees north of the equator—becomes an equally accomplished, successful and fulfilled wife, mother and grandmother at one and the same time, no less and then moves and completely adapts to the totally opposite climes of Minnesota.

Our desire is that readers—and we hope they number in the thousands—will enjoy these vignettes of the observations and work of a unique individual whose positive approach to her own circumstances provide inspiration and challenge to each and all of us. As you read, enjoy, laugh a lot, weep a little, may you be moved and grateful for the privilege and opportunity of shared insights from the life of a true Transition Woman.

Bill and Audrey Cowley
Birmingham, Alabama

WHEREVER HE LEADS

IN THE BEGINNING

Sitting in my bedroom, I found myself eagerly contemplating the future but saddened because it meant leaving my family. However, the die had been cast and I had committed myself to a service that had been tugging at my heart for years.

That gentle tugging began during my school-teaching years but was put aside during World War II when, to do my duty for my country, I took a job in a defense plant that manufactured gunpowder. The end of the war and closing of the plant forced me to search deep down inside to choose between returning to teaching or answering the call that I had felt prior to the war. A call so strong at times that I found it almost impossible to sing the hymn "Wherever He Leads, I'll Go," during church services without my stomach twisting into knots.

Finally, it occurred to me to contact the Foreign Mission Board to ascertain if there would be interest in someone with my qualifications, which I seriously doubted. If not, I would feel at peace resuming my teaching career. I was shocked when the Foreign Mission Board's response stated, "PREPARE. WE NEED YOU!" As far as I was concerned, there could be no clearer message from the Lord.

"Preparation" meant obtaining a M.R.E. (Masters of Religious Education) degree from the Southern Baptist Seminary in Louisville. I had only a few days to get registered for the fall semester.

Two years later, having obtained that degree, I and a few other mission volunteers from the Seminary purchased train tickets for Richmond, Va., home of the Foreign Mission Board. There, we would be assigned to a foreign field, then return home for a short period before saying a final good-bye to our families. I really didn't want to leave my family. We had always been very close, and I wouldn't see them for four years! But I also felt the message loud and clear. There could be no turning back.

I sought counsel with my pastor, the Rev. R. L. Puckett. "If it is the Lord's Will you will never be at peace with yourself unless you follow it," he said. "And if it isn't the Lord's Will, something will surely happen that you won't have to go." I agreed.

That evening, as I was musing over my future, the telephone rang. I was surprised to hear the voice of Bill Marshall of the Foreign Mission Board in Richmond. He told me I had failed the physical exam given to mission volunteers prior to assignment. This amused me, for I knew, without a doubt, that I had passed; I had never failed a physical in my entire life.

However, the doctor who did the psychiatric testing immediately came to mind. He had been determined to get me to admit that I wanted to go to a foreign land to escape an unrequited love affair. His efforts amused me at first. But his continued attempts to obtain an admission irritated me so much I called him "a Freudian psychiatrist!" However, nothing I said persuaded him that I was not trying to escape a disappointed love affair. If I had failed any portion of the examination, I felt it had to be with this psychiatrist. However, if this was the way the Lord chose to tell me I was NOT to go, then I was ready to accept it. A feeling of relief came over me that I hadn't experienced in months.

The next morning I cashed in my railway ticket on my way to the seminary.

The other mission volunteers had already heard my news.

"What are you going to do?" they inquired with concern.

— IN THE BEGINNING —

"I'm going back to teaching," I answered. "You see, we have literally thousands of teachers here, but in every country where we have missions, there are so few. That's the main reason I felt the Lord was calling me to service. But now it's apparent that He isn't and I gratefully accept it."

My family was overjoyed that I wasn't leaving.

The next evening, as I sat contemplating where to resume my teaching career, the phone rang. It was Bill Marshall again.

"Cora Ney," he said apologetically, "There's been a mistake. We want you to come on for an appointment!"

"Look," I said, "I've already cashed in my ticket. What do you folks think I am — a guinea pig to be tossed around and studied?"

We want you to talk with a psychiatrist here in Richmond," Marshall went on in a calm tone.

I was really in a dilemma now. Then I realized that Dr. Cornell Goerner, my missions professor at the seminary, was the only one who knew enough about our missions operation to provide the guidance I needed.

When we met the next day, I asked if he had talked with the Foreign Mission Board about me. And, if so, had he said anything that caused them to change their minds?

"No, Cora Ney," he replied, throwing both arms up in the air. "I haven't talked with anyone! But if they want you, you MUST go! The Lord has His hand in this!" I repurchased my ticket and left for Richmond.

At the Foreign Mission office, I learned from the Mission Board psychiatrist that the same doctor had "failed" all the other single women too. "When we received those reports, we KNEW something was wrong," he laughed. "Young lady, YOU are going to the mission field!" I was pleased, yet felt an even greater sadness than before because I had to tell my family all over again.

I had volunteered for China, but while I was at the seminary the Communists had gained control there and closed all doors to missionaries. Because the need for teachers was so great in Nigeria, they asked me to consider going there. At the seminary I had learned that Nigeria was a British Colony in western Africa, situated practically on the equator, which meant a hot and humid climate.

"I am not eager to leave my country for any foreign one," I replied, "but" — recalling that hymn I'd struggled with so often, "if I'm needed in Nigeria, then it's there I will gladly go."

They asked me to leave as soon as possible because they needed teachers there so badly. I went home to make ready. Those last few days were filled with excitement, good-byes, tears and anticipation. And, of course, so many questions:

"Why does a young lady like you want to waste her life in Africa?"

"Will you be out among the cannibals and headhunters?"

"Will you be sleeping in a tree house so you can be up away from the wild animals?"

"How deep in the jungle will you be?"

"Are there vaccines for all those strange diseases they have over there?"

A question that really stumped me, one I hadn't given the slightest thought to, was asked by a lady from my sponsoring church in Campbellsville, Ky.:

"Will you be permitted to wear lipstick over there?"

My response was the same to all inquiries: "I have absolutely no idea. I only know I am going out there to teach!"

The train trip to New York from Louisville was extremely sad for me. I had just said good-bye to my father, my sister, my two brothers and my four-year-old nephew, Winston Hardy, whom I'm afraid I had spoiled terribly. He could not understand why I would leave him.

The Mission Board handled all the travel arrangements. In New York I was put on an Air France plane to Paris. I spent one night there, then another Air France plane took me to the capitol city of Nigeria, Lagos, located right on the Atlantic Ocean.

I expected it to be a long, tiring, and because of my lack of French, silent trip. As we took off I caught a glimpse of the Statue of Liberty. This caused a huge lump in my throat, something that always happened thereafter whenever I caught a glimpse of that wonderful lady holding her torch so high in the sky.

A nice looking, well-mannered young man sat next to me, but was not talkative. During a meal, I learned he had served in Europe during the war and was returning to marry a French girl.

I was "spitting cotton" for a drink of water, but every time I asked, they brought wine. Finally, the young man said "If you would let me have the wine they bring you, I believe I can get you some water."

"I'll be glad to let you have all the wine they bring for a glass of good water," I replied.

He yelled at a stewardess, "BRING THIS LADY A BOTTLE OF WATER!" As if his words were magic, a beautiful, refreshing-looking bottle of water immediately appeared on my tray. And if it wasn't the best I'd ever tasted, it certainly was most welcome.

In Paris I was apprehensive about being alone and out of my

own country for the first time, but it was so good to feel the soft sheets of the bed that I instantly fell into a deep, energizing sleep.

After my very first continental breakfast the following morning, I was off to the airport again. I checked in and sat in the waiting room reading a book. Suddenly, I felt eyes staring at me. I looked up, and was surprised to see a huge, dark man standing in front of me. I was even more surprised when he asked, "Miss Hardy, you're going to Lagos, aren't you?" How did he know my name? How did he know where I was going?

I answered "Yes," curtly, and returned to my book.

He sat down directly across from me, still looking at me intently.

"Do you have someone meeting you in Lagos?" he asked.

I replied that I did and continued reading, although my concentration was not very good. Each time I looked up he was peering at me. That he knew my name and where I was going and wanted to know if I was being met, coupled with his disturbing mannerisms, left no doubt in my mind about his intentions. I was one American girl, in a foreign country for the first time, who was not about to be "picked up" by a foreigner.

But I wondered just how I was going to escape his advances.

My thoughts were interrupted by the loudspeaker announcing my flight to Lagos. I gathered my belongings and stood up as the announcement continued, in several languages: "ALL WOMEN AND CHILDREN WILL BE BOARDED FIRST." The English words were welcome to my ears and they provided my manner of escape.

Boarding, I quickly sat next to a nice-looking young girl whom, I learned, was a Briton on her way to marry a fiancé who worked for the British government in Lagos.

In the Beginning

The men boarded and, sure enough, this huge, dark stranger took the seat directly across the aisle from me. He made several attempts to strike up a conversation but I made every effort to be talking with the British girl. He finally gave up, and we settled in for the flight to Lagos, where I would be spending at least the next four years.

We disembarked in Lagos, cleared customs, and I looked for the missionaries who were supposed to meet me. They were not there. A late departure from Paris and earlier-than-expected arrival in Lagos had obviously messed up my plans. I found I was alone and the weather was exactly as expected — hot and humid!

The huge, dark man approached me again. Removing his hat, he said politely, "Miss Hardy, my driver is here and it doesn't appear that your friends are here to meet you."

I replied, "No, and I can't imagine what has happened to the missionaries who were to meet me."

"I bet you're with the Baptist Mission, aren't you?" he asked, wrinkling his balding forehead.

I acknowledged that I was and felt he must know something about the Mission.

"I know where the Baptist hostel is," he said, "And I'll be happy to drop you off there on my way."

I felt it unwise to stay in the small airport alone when everyone else seemed to be leaving. And since he knew about our Baptist Mission and might well be a friend of some of our missionaries, I accepted his offer. His driver put my luggage in the car and got into the back seat. The man got under the wheel, located on the right side. (It was the first British-made vehicle I had seen.) I took the front passenger seat.

During the trip I learned that he was Lebanese, from Beirut, with a business in Lagos. He had obtained my name from the passenger list. As we reached the city limits he began honking the horn — HONK! HONK! HONK! — almost continuously. I thought he must be a little crazy as the incessant noise wore on my nerves. I later learned that you could easily hit someone unless you honked continuously. If you came close, they yelled, "Why didn't you honk?"

It was a great relief when he finally stopped in front of a gate through which a sign on one of the buildings read "BAPTIST HOSTEL." I had arrived.
And in one piece! He politely helped me out of the car and took my luggage to the hostel door. We rang the bell and he patiently waited until a slovenly-attired lady, looking as if she had just awakened from a deep sleep, opened the door.

I thanked him and said good-bye. He tipped his hat and left. I never saw him again. But whatever would I have done had he not been there?

"Hello, don't tell me you're Cora Ney Hardy," the lady said. "We were expecting you later tonight. I'm Alice Griffin and you'll have to excuse the way I look!" Her gracious greeting was oh, so very welcome!

She explained that the airport had notified them that my plane had been delayed in Paris and would arrive later in the evening, "so all the other missionaries have gone to the beach for a picnic dinner."

As Alice helped me to my room, I couldn't help but be amused. A PICNIC DINNER AT THE BEACH! INDEED! This was certainly not the lifestyle I had expected in the mission field. I regret-

— IN THE BEGINNING —

ted Alice's headache, but how fortunate she didn't go to the beach, for the house would have been empty and I would still be at the mercy of that Lebanese man.

When I looked at Alice, one of the questions asked at home was answered. I could not wear lipstick here.. Her face bore not a trace of makeup.

I removed my lipstick and, after a short rest, went to the living room. Alice soon came in, looking neat and prim, and SHE WAS WEARING LIPSTICK! So I went to my room and reapplied mine. When the missionaries returned, Alice told them how embarrassed she was that I had caught her in such dishevelment. I laughed and told MY side of the story. It rapidly spread all over the mission field and remains, even today, a story often repeated when missionaries from Nigeria gather.

SURPRISE! SURPRISE! SURPRISE!

Before I left for Nigeria, Susan Anderson, principal of our Baptist Teacher Training College in Abeokuta, Nigeria (who was home on furlough), told me that I would probably be stationed at her school. So I was surprised to learn that my first job would be teaching at the girls' primary school in Yaba, a suburb of Lagos. Lagos was by far the largest city in Nigeria. This was fine with me; I had resolved to go anywhere I was needed.

One of the first couples I met were the Adairs, who had been in the Nigerian Mission field for ten years. J. B. was business manager of the Nigerian Mission, a busy job, because all mission personnel, materials, equipment and everything else came through Lagos. His wife, Odessa, was principal of the Reagan Memorial Baptist Girls' School where I would be teaching, a school that by American standards was the equivalent of grades one through eight. They were among the missionaries at the beach when I arrived. They took me to their home in Yaba to live for two weeks, until the annual Missions Meeting. At the meeting I would "definitely be assigned" a permanent position.

Their home on the Reagan Memorial School compound was a two-story single family residence with all the modern conveniences I was accustomed to in the States, with the exception of warm water, which was heated outside and carried into the house. Although far from extravagantly furnished, it was attractive and comfortable — quite different from what I had pictured as my home in the "African Jungle" — and a far cry from the tree house someone back home had suggested.

— SURPRISE! SURPRISE! SURPRISE! —

The Adairs were a Texas couple in their thirties, with a four-year-old son, Kenny, who seemed happy I was to be the new "boarder." He helped bridge the gap of my leaving my four-year-old nephew with whom I'd spent so many joyful days back home.

A visit to the school was first on the agenda. The following morning I met the African headmaster, Mr. Akapo, toured classrooms, was introduced to students and teachers and got my first look at the British educational system. When we entered a classroom, students rose in unison, said "Good morning, Ma," in perfectly good English., and remained standing until we left. I couldn't help but be amused as I asked myself, "Can't you just see our American students exhibiting such politeness?"

The students were neatly attired in white blouses with purple skirts — their school dress — and their smiling, shiny-clean faces made me feel most welcome.

I returned to the Adairs' home' for lunch feeling my future would be both challenging and rewarding. My fellow teachers, the students and the facilities were far superior to anything I had envisioned. During lunch the Adairs told me they were leaving on furlough within two months. It had not occurred to me that my new supervisor would not be there during my first year when everything was new to me. But this was nothing compared to Odessa's next surprise.

She said she had no intention of returning to the school in any capacity. She wanted to stay home and raise a family. If I had been in the mission field longer, her decision would not have been a surprise. Most of the wives held no positions, feeling that mission work was the responsibility of their husbands.

While I was chewing on this bit of information, she fired yet another volley.

"We wanted you here so that, hopefully, you can take over as principal at Reagan!" she explained. I gulped down the food in my mouth.

Three surprises, each greater than the previous one, were sufficient for my first lunch in Nigeria. However, an even greater one was yet to come.

Two weeks later at the Annual Missions meeting — compulsory for all missionaries — the Adairs' plans were adopted and I was officially made principal at Reagan. This meant much had to be learned in a very short time! The first order of business was to call a meeting of the school's Board of Governors. This board was similar to a Board of Education in the States: It guided the school's development and operation. I hoped we would all get to know each other better. To my surprise, the Board unanimously agreed that Reagan School be expanded from a primary into a primary AND secondary school — which meant adding six grades, equivalent to a high school in the States.

This expansion meant an extraordinary amount of additional work, first learning, and then satisfying, the British Codes and Standards. However, one aspect of obtaining approval from the British was easier for us than other schools because we were self-funding and required no monies from them. Without the Lottie Moon Christmas Offering at home, this would never have been possible!

Mrs. Adair resigned after the School Board's decision and in a few weeks they left on furlough. Few were surprised when they did not return a year later.

— SURPRISE! SURPRISE! SURPRISE! —

I burned an enormous amount of "midnight oil" planning and scheduling the work involved in a full secondary-school addition: Establishing the curriculum, identifying the entrance exams graduating eighth-graders must take and pass to gain eligibility for secondary school, the contractual and engineering plans for the buildings, seeking qualified staff to teach and numerous other activities, all the while maintaining the high standards of the primary school.

The School Board decided one additional secondary level would be added each year. I needed more time to become familiar with the British Educational System, but, after all, in the mission field one has little time for anything but carrying out what has been assigned, to the best of one's ability.

A new building had to be started immediately and it had to include a science lab, library and, at a minimum, three additional classrooms. Fortunately, we had a missionary who had been a builder by trade, and he drew up plans and started construction at once. Completion of the building, including all the equipment inside, required about a year — just in time for the first new class. For every project there are times of frustration, doubts and complications, and we experienced our share of each. However, when the new building was dedicated we were all — faculty, students, Board members and parents — a very proud group. Smiling faces were the order of the day.

One last obstacle to be conquered was an entrance exam formulated by the faculty from various other secondary schools' entrance exams. Quite a few of our graduating primary-school girls wanted to take the secondary-school entrance exam, which pleased me, because we wanted as many of our own girls to go on to the secondary-school level as possible. Nigerian educational law required that the exams be made available to all qualified students, from other schools as well as our own. Our teaching staff, although confident of our girls' abilities to pass, were just as concerned about how many would do so.

As the date for the exams grew closer, tension mounted for both the faculty and the girls themselves. Such an achievement would be a significant milestone for any 14-year-old Nigerian girl. There was nothing with which to compare such an achievement in the States. After all, Nigerian girls were only expected to become housewives, child bearers and laborers for their husbands.

All 16 of our girls who took the exams passed with marks at or near the top. From the shouts and cheers of our faculty, one would have thought we had just won the Super Bowl. I was especially pleased because I wanted only the very best for our first secondary-school class. Ten students from other schools were also accepted, making a total of 26 students in our first class.

I felt satisfaction and tremendous relief, knowing the job of expanding into secondary school was well on its way.

THE "BUSH"!

>Pussy cat, Pussy cat, where have you been?
>"I've been to London to see the King!"
>Pussy cat, Pussy cat, what did you there?
>"I frightened a little mouse under his chair!'

This nursery rhyme bears little resemblance to my initial visit to "see the King." In fact, if something as tender as a little mouse had been sighted in this King's court, it would probably have been captured and quickly converted to food.

Later, when I heard African-American youth back home proudly proclaim their family's descendants to be from African "royalty," it amused me somewhat and made me wonder if they really knew about African "royalty" and how it existed.

"What's that you say?" one of our missionaries, Homer Brown, frowned and yelled to me. "You've been in Nigeria this long and haven't been in the Bush yet? Well, we've got to get you educated about Africa. Why, you haven't seen anything yet."

Developing additional grade levels — all this and more — had kept my time at a premium. But this was between semesters and, regardless of time restraints, I was going into the Bush to see a different kind of Africa. I looked forward to getting away as well as to experiencing the Bush. I'd heard so many stories from other missionaries about their encounters out there and I wanted to see it all for myself. "Bush" was a quick, short, but totally accurate term for the African interior, or the "backwoods" as we might say in America. Nigerian tribal people still inhabited those areas and most of the Bush was still quite primitive.

The tribe we visited was in western Nigeria about 50 miles west of the Niger River. Shaki was the closest village. They spoke the Yoruba dialect, the dominant language in southwestern Nigeria. Most of the Reagan Memorial students spoke this language but, as with other languages, there were slightly different dialects and colloquialisms in the same language. Although Muslim was the dominant religion in this area, numerous gods and religions held sway in Bush country.

We motored through Abeokuta, Ibadan, Iwo and Ogbomosho, then drove into the Bush as far as we could and went the rest of the way on foot. Oh, how I enjoyed meeting other missionaries as we stopped in each town — in some we had hospitals, in others we had schools, etc. I had already met most of them as they entered Nigeria through Lagos or came there for meetings or supplies. Others I'd met at our Nigerian Convention. They all smiled that same "you'll find out" smile when they learned this was my first trip into the Bush.

— THE "BUSH"! —

When we left Ogbomosho, I got my first taste of "dressing for the Bush." Pantyhose were new then and had not been widely accepted back in the States. The kind I wore were constructed of heavy material, to help avoid sticks and bramble. I wore a split skirt of khaki that came well below my knees and a long-sleeved khaki shirt. Two entirely new items — for me — were boots that laced up to my knees. My brothers wore similar ones in their younger days. They were quite uncomfortable at first, but I was told I'd be very thankful for them when we started tramping through the Bush. And you know something? They were absolutely right!

Topping off my new wardrobe was a khaki-covered pith helmet. Looking at myself in a small mirror, it was difficult to believe it was really me! "If only the folks back home could see me now!" I chortled. Homer's wonderful wife, Millie, was in our traveling party and she was both my tutor and mind-leveler. I was so grateful she was along, but then I wouldn't have gone without her. By "mind leveler" I refer to the peace of mind she lent when the two men tried to make me ill at ease, something they did to all first-time Bush travelers, especially women. For example, when we left Ogbomosho I was told, "Now you better load up on this good food because it's the last time you'll have it until we return. You'll get used to 'monkey meat' and 'reptile grits' when we move into Bush country, especially when we reach the King (Oba was that tribe's name for him) and his people."

Millie's quick wink told me this was the type of needling every new Bush traveler had to experience. I smiled and ignored most of it, excepting when Jared Richardson, a doctor who had recently assumed a position as official contact for this tribe, asked, "Do you think you'll like monkey meat? Oh, I know you will. Everyone does, once they've tasted it."

"Sure she will," Homer chimed in.

This teasing continued until I finally had enough.

"Listen, you two," I said, "I will try anything to eat once. But as for eating monkey meat, as you call it, well, you two can have my share. I'll do without."

Both men laughed and my quick glance to Millie met with her approving nod, as if to say, "That's telling them!"

By late afternoon, we'd gone as far as the Lorrie (a Jeep, to Americans) could take us because of brush, trees and marshy ground. After an hour on foot, we made camp for the night, setting up one tent for Millie and me and another for the two men. We sat around the campfire after our meal, and I experienced my first indescribably-beautiful Bush sunset. It's gorgeous reddish-orange glow reflected on all the foliage, as well as our clothes and skin. I remarked, as we watched in quiet contentment, "Now I can understand what some people meant when they said they'd fallen in love with Africa, particularly the jungle part." Everyone nodded in agreement.

I hadn't realized how serenely quiet it would be that night, with only the sounds from various animals and other living things that reside in the Bush. But I was so tired it didn't take long to fall asleep.

Sunlight piercing the mesh window of our tent awoke me, along with noise made by seemingly thousands of birds and the sound of the men stirring the fire outside. We had bacon and eggs for breakfast, more delicious than I had ever tasted. Of course, Homer warned us, "Better enjoy while you can; we'll not be having anything like this for lunch."

Within a few minutes we'd made our backpacks and were tramping on towards the native village.

Our work to convert the tribes to Christianity consisted of several approaches, all directed, at first, toward helping the African help himself. In this instance, our evangelists and preachers had made initial contact several years earlier. Once the lines of distrust and fear had been dented, they called in our engineers to locate and drill for water. River or small-stream water was almost always filled with bacteria that caused sickness, frequent fevers and deaths. At least three wells had been dug and fresh water had helped lower illness and death rates significantly. At present, our engineers were working on methods to dispose of water and waste.

Another way to reach primitive people, such as these, for Jesus was to teach them proper hygiene techniques. Our medical people had made good progress with the tribe we were on our way to see, but much more was needed. Jared and his wife, also a doctor, were involved in this part of our work.

Yet another method, of course, was the way I was involved — teaching and educating them. This was usually a later step, because under-nourished, often ill and fearful people are much more difficult to teach and they learn very slowly, if at all.

Within an hour, I encountered two extraordinary sights.

The first was a giant ant hill, five- to six-feet-tall and easily three feet in diameter. I had seen ant hills around Lagos — usually a foot or so high, and since we had nothing like that in the States, I had marveled at them. But to see one of this magnitude — taller than I — was truly astounding.

"These are not the 'driver' ants you might have heard about," Jared said. 'Driver ' ants are vicious. They march along in long columns like an army, with soldier ants on each side of the column to protect it and the other ants inside, forming the interior of the column. They destroy anything in their way — eating it or killing it and tossing it aside. They have actually destroyed entire villages of people in their path. Even an animal as large as an elephant will avoid them if it can!"

I'd heard about them before, but still puzzled by their power, I asked, "Well, how do you fight them or stop them? Are they unstoppable?"

"It's very difficult to do," Jared said. "Chemicals have been developed that either kill them or render them helpless, but they put up a tremendous fight. They're still extremely dangerous and widely feared."

The huge ant hill seemed less formidable when I compared it to the powers of "driver" ants.

A little farther into the Bush we all stopped simultaneously, glaring at an object tied about four or five feet high on a sturdy bush. Homer and Jared motioned Millie and me over to it. It seemed to be a "mishmash" of several things: A couple of small pieces of cloth, a small piece of metal, various herbs, weeds and sticks, along with other unidentifiable items, all tied together with what looked like string but was a tough type of vine.

"There," Homer said, pointing, "I guess you know what that is, don't you?" He looked at me. I thought for a moment, but could not recall hearing or reading about any type of unusual "corsage" like the one in front of us.

'No, I don't.'

"That's a JUJU!" he smiled.

I'd heard that word before, but didn't know what it meant. I looked at Millie and she was nodding as if she knew.

"Well," Homer continued, "you might call it a sort of 'curse' someone tried to place on an enemy who they want the evil spirit, or their god, to harm."

"What do all those junky parts mean?" Millie asked.

"Oh, I can't tell you anything about that," Homer said, and referred the conversation to Jared.

"Each part has a special significance," Jared explained, "to the one who has placed the JUJU as well as to the one who is being cursed."

Taking a stick, Jared broke up the JUJU and watched it fall to the ground as he continued. "I've heard that if something that belonged to the person on whom the JUJU is being placed can be made a part of the JUJU itself, that makes it much more powerful, or so they believe."

Pointing to the scraps of fabric now on top of some weeds, he asked, "You see these small pieces of cloth and the piece of metal that were parts of it?"

We nodded, "Yes."

"These might belong to the one being cursed. I also understand that sometimes the JUJU takes the form of a doll made to look like the one on whom the JUJU has been placed. This is supposed to be very effective."

Leaving the fallen JUJU to its JUJU-ing, we walked on into the Bush until some tribal boys began to appear through the brush and trees. Most of them gave signs of greeting with waves and big smiles. They recognized Jared and Homer because of their previous trips to the village. Millie and I were given a more serious surveillance.

At the village several of them came up to us, laughing and extending signs of welcome, such as motioning us onward. We stopped momentarily to return welcome signs and to take a look at some of the activities of the women, then continued toward the King's residence. Anything else would have been considered impolite. I was eagerly trying to imagine what he and his residence would be like when we stopped in front of a rather small, ugly and dirty mud hut. Marks and symbols had been painted over the entrance with ink or stain. (Could it be blood, I wondered?)

Immediately two young men, perhaps 20 years of age, came from behind the hut and raised their hands for us to halt. They stood for a moment between us and the door, in no way intimidating or belligerent, then they disappeared inside.

"They must go in and usher the King (Oba) out," I was told.

A moment later, out they came, each with a hand under the arm of a shriveled-up, very old man. The King's eyes were almost completely closed and his body and clothes were filthy. He could hardly stand, let alone walk, and I wondered if he could see.

Another young villager hastened up with a cone-shaped object and, after a bit of ceremony, placed it on the King's head. Yet another young man put a string of beads around his neck. The necklace appeared to be made of bones, stones and sticks. "That's his crown and royal covering," Jared whispered to Millie and me.

A few moments later we were sitting almost in a circle. Millie and I sat on two large rocks. The King, his retinue, Jared and Homer all sat on mats that were brought from the King's hut and unrolled and ceremoniously laid out on the ground in front of his hut. Millie and I were introduced and the King bowed his head to us and tried to form a smile. When he learned that Millie was Homer's wife, he raised a hand and in a loud voice repeatedly uttered something.

— THE "BUSH"! —

"That's right," Homer nodded approvingly. "Christians need only one wife, only one!" All the men nodded to each other in agreement. Turning to us, Homer explained that one of the hardest things to convince the King to do, so he could become a Christian, was to give up two of his three wives.

Jared asked how the two women were doing. "Odaye," the King said, which meant they were doing fine. Later, I learned that two unmarried tribal men and taken them for wives. Any man in the tribe would consider it an honor and a duty to marry either one of them because she had been a wife of the King.

I was introduced as one who teaches young girls to make them better women and Christians, and the old man strained his eyes towards me, clasped his hands and muttered, "G-o-o-o-d. G-o-o-o-d." This eased my mind somewhat.

Then we met some of the children and a few of the women, who showed us what they had been making as we entered the village. Finally, it was "lunch" time, and my stomach began a slow, anticipative turn. Some villagers disappeared behind the King's hut. Millie and I, to get a better look, stepped off at an angle where we could watch the food preparation.

"Just like in the movies," she whispered, as we watched "lunch" cooking in a huge black pot hanging over a wood fire on the ground. Jared came up behind us, while Homer and the King continued a discussion. "You'll find it's like a soup or a stew," he told us, "usually made from vegetables and herbs. Sometimes it contains meat.'"

"Monkey-meat!'" I thought, but said nothing.

Millie told me later that the same thing came instantly to her mind. Jared smiled and added, "No, it won't be 'monkey-meat.' They consider wild boar a real delicacy. Or perhaps they've added a piece of beef. But most likely it will be either chicken or some kind of meaty bird."

We returned to our seats on the rocks. The King was served first. He picked up a gourd that was cut in half with the larger end hollowed out and sun-dried to form a large spoon. His food was in a larger, hollowed-out dried gourd. He ceremoniously tasted it and nodded approvingly to his servers. He then waited until all of us were served before slowly raising both hands with open palms to the sky. Then he peered upwards and pronounced a few words softly, blessing the food. He looked at Homer and Jared. They, along with all of us, bowed their heads and said grace, ending with a request to the Lord to continue to bless the King and his people. The King took the next spoonful of food and then we all began to eat. "Its good," Jared told our host.

"G-o-o-o-d!" repeated the King, raising spoonful after spoonful to his lips.

Together, Millie and I dipped our spoons into our bowls. The contents appeared to be vegetables and/or herbs, as Jared had predicted. Mostly, though, it was juice. I tasted it and rolled it around inside my mouth, measuring its consistency and flavor, then swallowed. Millie did the same and looked to see my reaction. I gave none. Neither did she.

I'd never tasted anything quite like it, before or since. We both managed to eat about half of our portions. That was sufficient. I braced myself for the onslaught I was certain my stomach would make, but it didn't. Good old "cast-iron" intestines! Just another requisite for a missionary.

After lunch, Jared and Homer took Bibles out of their backpacks, pointing out that they had just been translated and printed in

Yoruba. They presented them to the King who was obviously pleased with the gift. Homer told him that two boys from his village who had entered one of our schools were off to a good start and would make good students. This also seemed to please the King immensely. He smiled so openly that I could see most of the interior of his mouth. He had no teeth. No wonder we had soup for lunch, I thought. He couldn't have eaten anything else!

By mid-afternoon, at the day's hottest and most humid, Homer gathered us in a circle and, holding hands, with some of the villagers joining in, led us in a parting prayer. Then the King stumbled his way to Millie and me, stopped, reached toward us and, in turn, placed his hands on our shoulders and smiled..

He's giving you his royal blessing," Jared whispered. We returned his smile and did a short bow. "This means you are always welcome in his village."

Then two young boys from his court handed crosses to Millie and me. They were only crude sticks tied together with twine or vines, but we both were touched and thanked the boys and the King, then waved an appreciative hand to the villagers. It made my day.

As we began our homeward journey, young boys followed us for a while, just as they had met us, waving whenever we looked toward them. Of course, we waved back.

The return trip seemed longer and more arduous because we were very tired, but I couldn't get those people out of my mind. I felt a rejuvenated spirit swelling up inside me. Our missions' effort suddenly took on a more encompassing vision. I kept realizing over and over that these people who were so gracious to us would never have heard about our Lord Jesus Christ except for the work of our missionaries. And our missionaries wouldn't be there

Cora Ney with her monkey friend

were it not for the concern and love of our people and churches back home.

In the hectic days at my school I had somehow failed to see the scope and totality of our foreign-missions effort. Now I realized for the first time that this was a much-needed trip. It had provided me with renewed energy and commitment. Suddenly, the world seemed smaller than it had ever seemed to me before as Jesus' words, "Go ye into all the world, preaching the Gospel to all peoples" (Mark 16:15) took on added emphasis. It was not just a request, it was a command.

AND DOWN IT CAME!

Joyce Kilmer's famous poem, "Trees," has always been one of my favorites. I certainly agree with the opening lines, "I think that I shall never see/ a poem lovely as a tree."

A mighty kapok tree towered over a hundred feet in the air in a corner of the school compound, providing an abundance of shade. In season, it bore fruit of white, cotton-like fibers that was used to stuff pillows, mattresses, etc. Because of its beauty, I was distressed when Josiah, my head man, told me a gardener had reported that its trunk was beginning to rot. I contacted several offices seeking advice, but received none.

Soon afterward, the Senior Officer of Education from the British office in Lagos appeared at my office door and said, "Good morning, Miss Hardy. I see you have a problem tree out here."

"You mean the kapok tree, which is rotting?"

He nodded.

"I don't know quite what to do about it," I said. "I contacted the Forestry Department, hoping they could advise me. But they knew of nothing to do with a tree like that once it started to rot."

"You'd better have that tree cut," he warned, raising a finger .

"Who would be able to cut it?" I asked.

"I don't think there's anybody in Nigeria who could cut it," he said.

I was puzzled and irritated. "That's a strange thing. You tell me to have it cut, then tell me there's no one in Nigeria who can cut it?" Finally, I looked him straight in the eye and asked, "What can I do.?"

He thought for a moment. "Well, if you allow it to stand and a storm comes along it will fall, and if it falls in one of three directions, you could have a serious lawsuit on your hands!"

I told him I would see what I could do, not knowing where to turn.

He suggested I call the Railway Department because they employed men to keep trees and brush away from the rail tracks. Perhaps they could offer assistance or suggestions. Then he took time to visit some of the classrooms and was on his way. His parting words were, "BE SURE TO TAKE CARE OF THAT TREE!"

I called the railway office and asked if anyone could help me. "We have no one qualified or capable of handling a job such as that," the railway officer said. No matter whom I contacted, I received almost the identical response.

One fascinating thing about the tree was that roots grew out from the trunk about four feet above the ground, then grew down the trunk to the ground and spread out approximately four more feet around the base before growing down into the ground. It resembled a giant centipede with the eight tangled-tight roots growing out from its base like a centipede's legs.

Before we bought the land and fenced in the whole compound, pagan worshippers brought bowls of grain and small insects, built fires and made sacrifices to the tree. It had become one of their idols. However, the fence put an immediate stop to such rituals.

Finally, in desperation, I again called the Mission Office for help. The director said, "Cora Ney do the best that you can!" This changed my desperation to bewilderment and also a bit of anger.

I called Josiah and asked if he knew of anyone we could get to cut down the tree. "I will talk to the gardener. I will find somebody!" he assured me. ""Don't you worry! I'll find somebody!"

His assurances did little to relieve the tension and stress building up inside me.

However, several days later Josiah brought in a diminutive, white-haired African who couldn't have weighed over 130 pounds. He introduced him as "Jida, the man I have gotten to cut down the tree." They both smiled huge smiles.

I asked Jida if he would cut it down limb by limb, which I felt was the only possible way to do it and avoid demolishing any of the buildings surrounding it.

He assured me the tree would come down precisely that way.

"How much will you charge," I asked.

"One hundred pounds," he shot back.

One hundred pounds at that time amounted to about 400 American dollars, which I thought was a terribly high price. But I doubted that I could find anyone else to do it. I agreed to pay him once the tree was safely down and disposed of.

Several days later Jida returned with four men and they began to saw, not limb by limb, as promised, but down at the trunk about two feet above the ground. They used long saws with men manning the handles at each end. Sawing through the maze of roots took an inordinate amount time.

But what upset me was that he had not started by removing the limbs, one at a time. I asked why. He claimed that this was a better way, which added to my frustration.

I called the two missionary couples in our station and they came at once, but did nothing except stand and fearfully watch as the Africans continued to saw on the giant tree.

The Lebanese Counselor lived on one side of my compound, and if the tree fell in that direction his residence would be crushed.

I decided to warn him. He politely explained that his wife had just delivered a new baby and simply "wasn't up to" leaving the house!

The Leventis Company's Nigerian offices were on another side. They seemed totally unconcerned.

The third direction, our school compound, was the least of my worries at the moment.

The fourth direction was the only way the tree could fall without causing damage.

Each rip of the saw seemed to be ripping away my insides.

When they got about halfway through the trunk, Jida and his men started putting away their saws. The watching missionaries alerted me. We hastened to the gate and stood in front of it, and I told Jida they could NOT leave until that tree had come down. They resumed sawing without argument and the missionaries stayed at the gate to see that no one left.

A few hours later I heard cracking and popping, then a tremendous "SWISH" as the tree hit the ground. My knees almost buckled under me. How had it fallen? Which direction? Was there any damage? Had anyone been hurt? With these questions surging through my mind I ran outside. My prayers had been answered! The tree had fallen in the safe direction. I felt as if the weight of the entire continent of Africa had been lifted from my shoulders.

I thought Jida would saw the tree up and haul it away. But when the group returned the next day, with two additional helpers, they began to dig a trench alongside the fallen tree. They went down about six feet, then rolled the tree into the trench and began sawing off branches and dropping them down alongside the trunk. I had thought the tree would be valuable to them, but apparently kapok doesn't make the best firewood.

When they finished, Jida came to my office for his pay. But first we walked out to the site. It was impossible to tell that a tree trunk was anywhere under the ground, they had shoveled dirt back over the top and smoothed it out so well. Only a two-foot high stump remained.

Never had I been happier to pay 100 pounds for a job so well done. As I handed Jida his check, I thanked him and told him how pleased I was. He smiled broadly, revealing snaggled teeth, thanked me, bowed politely, turned and left, thus ending an experience I never wanted to repeat.

TO SCARED TO SPEAK

Peggy Marchman, a missionary friend visiting from up country, rushed into my bedroom at approximately 2:30 in the morning and whispered frantically, "Cora Ney! Thieves are downstairs.!"

Forgetting that my new pink mosquito net was tucked in tightly around my bed, I leaped up and out, splitting it from top to bottom. No matter! We rushed to the top of the stairs and I took a quick step downward.

Peggy grabbed my arm and whispered, "Don't you dare go down there!"

"But I must! They'll carry out everything I have!"

From the stories told by robbery victims, that is exactly what thieves did. It wasn't going to happen here if I could help it! I rushed down to the first landing and, as I looked across the hallway through the dining-room doorway, the moonlight revealed several human forms working at the French doors that led from the verandah into the dining room.

Peggy and I were still safe, but once the thieves got inside the house, anything could happen, including physical harm. Somehow, they had to be stopped immediately. One or two possibilities skipped through my mind, but didn't seem adequate.

Desperately I tried to yell "KI LO FE" (pronounced "key low fay"), which means "What do you want?"

But I could produce absolutely no sound, no matter how hard I tried! Never had I felt so helpless and terrified! Finally, I made a gigantic effort and, to my surprise, produced a sound loud enough to be heard!

The forms on the verandah were motionless for just a moment, a moment that seemed an eternity. Then, back out through the verandah doors they scampered, across the lawn and into the darkness created by palm trees on that side of the compound.

The top bolt on the French doors was broken and the middle bolt was on the verge of giving way. I called out repeatedly to our night watchman, but there was no response., so I called the police. The station was only a block away and two uniformed Nigerians arrived in a few minutes.

"Where is your night watchman?" was their first question.
"I don't know," I replied. "I have called him but he does not answer!"

"We'll find him," they assured me.

They found him asleep on the verandah of a nearby school building and brought him back to my verandah, where the robbery had been attempted.

They stood him up by the door with a nightstick under his chin and told him, "We're going to put you here and you'd better not leave! If anybody gets into this house tonight, we're holding you responsible!" He was fully awake and most cooperative.

Turning to Peggy and me, they assured us, " We'll be by here often to see to it that no one comes around again! You ladies go back to bed and don't worry. We'll see that you don't have thieves tonight!"

As we climbed the stairs, Peggy said, "Cora Ney, you were trying to make your voice sound like a man, weren't you?"

I laughed and replied, "Like a MAN? No, I was just trying to make it sound, PERIOD!"

The remainder of the night passed peacefully.

THE CHRISTMAS TREE

It was a magnificent tree made of shiny silver aluminum foil. As it shimmered in the lights, I was happy I had brought it back from my last home leave. It was a gift from my sister Margaret and her husband Roy. This made it even more special because I missed so terribly the Christmases I spent with them each time I was on furlough.

But my joy was nothing compared to the excitement of the schoolgirls and staff, who gazed at it at every opportunity with wide-eyed wonderment. MaMo, the dormitory matron, summed up the Africans' feelings when she marveled, "I think this must be what Heaven is going to look like!"

I was sitting in my roughly-hewn rocking chair enjoying the tree's peaceful atmosphere one evening before Christmas when a voice from the front gate interrupted the silence. "Please, Ma . . ."

I went to the verandah door to find the night watchman from Barclays' Bank, just across the street from our school.

"Please Ma, I believe your night watchman is in a fight down on the corner!"

Having handled our banking at Barclays' for a number of years and knowing their employees to be trustworthy, I rushed out and followed him. When we reached the corner, I saw two Africans wrestling and punching each other and sure enough, one was our own night watchman. Oh, how disgusted I was at such behavior.

"Musa!" I shouted, "Get back to our compound!"

He stopped immediately.

I walked rapidly back to the compound., and Musa followed reluctantly. The Barclays' Bank watchman returned to his post. On the verandah, I turned and locked the metal door as Musa came in the front gate. He walked up to the front door and, in an extremely loud voice, began demanding his pay and stating he was quitting. There is no need to explain, in detail, the exact words he used.

Suspecting that he was either on drugs or alcohol, I wouldn't open the door. In a firm tone, I said, "Musa, come back in the morning and I'll give you your salary and then you may leave."

He ran around the house but was soon back with an iron rod. He began banging it on the door, determined to get in.

"Stop it! Stop it immediately!" I yelled, but the banging continued. Fortunately, the door was made of metal and, although it bent slightly, I was confident it could not be broken down. The banging continued.

Josiah came running from his house and yelled at Musa to stop. I told Josiah what had happened. Perhaps because he was the oldest African employee on the compound and something of an "elder statesman" to the others, when Josiah told Musa to leave peacefully and return in the morning for his money, the night watchman heeded his advice.

Peace again descended upon the household.

The next day word of what had happened quickly spread throughout the school. Everyone was concerned. MaMo came rushing over the minute she heard. She looked at the front door, saw the bent metal bars, and exclaimed, "Oh, Ma! What if he had broken in? Why, he would have just ruined the Christmas tree!"

SEIDEI
(pronounced see-dee)

"What on earth do you mean?" I asked when I was told that the Priest of the Lagos, Nigeria, Muslim sect had requested an appointment.

What could he want of me? How did he know about me? My name?
Could there be a dispute of some kind emerging? Was he bringing an olive branch, a peace offering and, if so, why? These and other questions darted through my mind.

A date and time for our meeting were established through messengers, which was the custom, and I eagerly but apprehensively awaited his arrival. The moment came too soon.

I heard footsteps in the corridor and, looking up, saw two men in my doorway. Although I'd never met a Muslim, it was usual to see them in the city, particularly the marketplace. As the two — not one as I expected — entered, it was quite obvious from their dress that they were Muslims. Their colorful tunics, open sandals and full, ankle-length trousers identified them. I motioned for them to sit but both remained standing directly in front of my desk, looking down at me.

I was not going to rise after such a cold first encounter.

Finally, the Priest spoke in an expressionless voice: "My name is Mr. Agoyla and I am Priest of Islam at the Temple of Allah here in Lagos." His voice was deliberately slow and precise and his English was almost perfect. This surprised me.

He paused as if he expected a response but I only nodded. He continued in a demanding voice.

"I want my two daughters to come to this school. I have made inquiries throughout all of Western Africa, and I have learned that your school is the best one available for girls."

Again he paused, but I only nodded that I understood. A longer pause lasted until I decided to break the silence.

"We do accept students of all backgrounds, provided they can qualify to our standards and provided we have room for them."

The Principal's office at Reagan School

Silence prevailed again.

"You must understand," I continued, "that we are a Christian school, sponsored by Southern Baptists in the United States. In addition to educating our girls, we also hope to show them the way to becoming Christians."

The faces of both men remained expressionless.

"Have you considered that, by attending school here, your daughters might become Christians?" I asked.

"No," he quickly responded., with a defiant look. "I'm not afraid of that happening. They are Allah's children and have been reared to love Islam. I have absolutely no fear of them embracing any kind of infidel religion!"

My blood began to boil, but I had been trained, and also had learned when I came to the mission field, to accept insults, or worse, with a smile. That he wanted his daughters educated was most unusual for a Muslim, as well as for any African, because they almost unanimously believed it was useless to try to educate daughters. Girls just did not possess the ability to learn, in their opinion.

His confidence amused me but I tried not to show it. I explained, "First, please take these applications for admission with you, fill them out and return them to me within a week, along with the full application fee. Should your daughters not be admitted, for whatever reason, your money will be returned."

They took the forms, but said nothing, so I continued. "After the applications are reviewed by our staff, should they be favorably received, your daughters will have to take, and pass, an entry examination here at the school in order to qualify. Then, provided they pass and we have the room, you will receive all the pertinent information pertaining to their acceptance, along with instructions as to when and where they are to report, what clothes and personal property they can bring and all other needed information."

Mr. Agoyla's accomplice stepped aside, bowed to him, and made a broad sweep of his hand towards the door. Mr. Agoyla gave me one last blunt look, turned, and the two of them left abruptly.

The application forms were returned two days later. Both girls qualified and were admitted the next semester.

— SEIDEI —

During the first year, we quickly learned that Seidei, the eldest, was quite intelligent. She was also very pretty, with long flowing black hair, black eyes and a captivating smile. She not only excelled in class but was also outstanding in art, music and sports, which made her extremely popular with her classmates.

Wosulatu, the youngest, was not particularly interested in learning and made little effort. She barely passed and exerted only enough energy to do so. However, we enjoyed having both girls as students.

After two years, I found a note on my desk one morning from Seidei, asking if she could talk with me. This was not unusual. Young girls, away from home for the first time, often needed to discuss various subjects and problems. Our staff was always ready and more than willing to talk. I sent a note back saying "yes," and that afternoon Seidei's smiling face appeared in my doorway.

"Please Ma," she softly asked, "may I come in?"

As we talked, her ebullient personality slowly became more serious.

"I want to become a Christian," she said in almost a pleading manner.

I was not surprised, but quickly realized the consequences of such an action.

"What does your father think about this," I asked.

"He doesn't know," she whispered, looking down. "I haven't told him. I haven't told anyone."

We both sat for a moment, considering.

"Would you go and talk to him?" she asked. "Please, Ma?"

"First," I interjected, "I'd like to know why you want to become a Christian?"

"Because I know that our Lord and Savior, Jesus, came to earth to show us how to live. Then he was crucified for our sins, rose from the grave and is alive today, sitting at the right hand of God, the Father, in Heaven. I know that he has saved me from my sins. I know!"

A more heartfelt profession of faith I'd never heard, especially from one so young.

I assessed the situation carefully. Should I see her father to break the news or should I call upon one of our missionary preachers? After all, I reasoned, I'm a teacher, not a minister, and isn't this more a minister's job? Then I looked down into Seidei's trusting eyes set in that beautiful face, eyes that began to fill and overflow with tears.

Minister or teacher, I suddenly reasoned, it really doesn't matter. I'm a missionary for our Lord, Jesus Christ, and this opportunity was provided me by Him.

"Yes," I said, taking her in my arms. "If you arrange for the time and place, I'll be glad to talk with your father."

I'll never forget the look of relief that came over her little face.

Again, messengers handled the arrangements.

Two days later I drove our Lorrie to the Agoyla residence, an address in the middle of Lagos' bustling business district. I parked and made my way slowly to a white door adjacent to a rather large store. A peek inside through the store window revealed furniture, pictures, figurines, etc. The door to which my instructions directed me did not open into the store. I pulled a cord that went through the door that was affixed to an ornately carved wooden handle, and in a few seconds I heard it unlock.

I opened the door, stepped inside, and was climbing a flight of dimly-lit stairs when a man suddenly appeared at the top of the stairs. He was dressed entirely in white, including his turban and broad sash. He motioned for me to come on up, then gestured to his right (my left) to yet another door. He made no move to open it, so I reached for the handle, opened the door and we both entered. Then he led me, slowly, down a long hallway, 55 to 60 feet long, carpeted with Oriental rugs.

We passed many rooms, including a kitchen, dining room and many bedrooms, all elaborately furnished, mostly in the color jade, on both sides of the hall. I detected the scent of jasmine, and as we moved along the man in white still leading, the aroma became ever stronger but never to the extent of being offensive.

At the end of the hall was a lavishly-furnished sitting room, more brightly lighted than the other rooms we had passed. The man stopped and motioned for me to sit down. I chose a high-backed chair with large, cushioned arms, directly opposite the doorway. (I immediately recalled a western movie I'd seen in which the star always sat facing the door so he could see who was entering. Why such a thing came to me completely out of the blue, I didn't know, and I felt silly for remembering!")

My hands glided caressingly over the smooth, velvety upholstery, not at all like the simple furnishings at our school. The room was lined on three sides with all kinds, shapes, sizes and heights of sofas, seats and hassocks and in the center of it all was a large marble-topped table on which there were at least two dozen pictures of children — all different faces, including Seidei and Wosulatu — of various ages.

I wondered if they were all the Priest's children, for I seemed to recall that Muslims could have as many as four wives, all of equal standing, but only if they could afford them. In the center of the table was a huge green candle, unlit, so it couldn't be the source of the jasmine aroma. Although the furnishings were in many colors, jade was still dominant. I had been in several Lagos residences, but none as impressive as this.

Mr. Agoyla appeared in the archway, dressed in a bright yellow tunic with a long flowing red sash hanging from his shoulder. His face was again expressionless. He did not acknowledge my presence nor did he extend any form of welcome. He looked slowly around the room, then moved directly across from me and sat on a hassock, about a foot off the floor. Silence ruled.

Finally, he looked at me and said "Good afternoon."

I responded, with a polite smile. Silence again prevailed.

Not having all afternoon to sit there waiting for him to say something, I decided to get straight to the point.

"Mr. Agoyla," I tried to speak calmly, "Seidei has come to me to tell me she wants to become a Christian." There was no response, so I continued, looking directly into his blank face. "Will you permit her to do so?"

He dropped his head and, if the previous moments of silence were long ones, this seemed an eternity. At long last, he looked up and said, "Yes, if she wants to become a Christian, she may." His voice was soft but firm and disapproving.

I thanked him and said that I fully realized this was a difficult decision for him, and that I appreciated his permitting Seidei to do what she felt inside she had to do. I arose, said good-bye, and was led again by the white-clad servant down the hall to the door, descended the stairs and left.

Only three days were left until our week-long semester holiday and I expected Seidei to make her decision public at one of these last morning chapel services. When she didn't, I was concerned but not disappointed When classes resumed after the holiday, neither Seidei nor Wosulatu returned. Nor was there a call or note to inform us why. I began to feel that Mr. Agoyla had won the battle, but I didn't give up hope.

Two weeks later, a letter arrived from Seidei written on board a ship to London, where her father was sending them to another school. She wrote that she still wanted to become a Christian and was attending services on board ship. I believed her.

As years passed, I thought of Seidei many times, wondering where she might be and what she could be doing. One day I was in the business district and almost went into her father's store to inquire about her, but had neither the time nor the courage to do so.

Now, all missionaries in Nigeria, especially those in the extremely tropical climate of Lagos, were required to have a complete annual physical exam. Liking the way a fellow Kentuckian, Dr. Martha Gilliland, conducted her exams, I always compiled enough business matters to warrant a trip to Ogbomosho where she worked in one of our hospitals. After business was taken care of, I'd have my exam and we'd have lots of fun talking about our family and friends and any news from home. I always received a clean bill of health. The only thing of any consequence this time was a small mole under my left arm which sometimes interfered with my dressing. Martha burnt it off with a needle.

Rather than motor back to Lagos on a busy weekend, I stayed over and accompanied Martha to her church. Its practically 100% African congregation met in a structure very similar to others in southern Nigeria — every side except the front was open from floor to ceiling to let in as much fresh air as possible. I noticed a young mother with two children in an aisle we passed.

We sat down and I opened my Bible and began to read. I heard footsteps approaching and suddenly two feet were next to mine. Looking up, I saw the young mother and her children. She had a captivating smile I knew I had seen before but could not quite place.

"Miss Hardy?" she asked sweetly. "Miss Hardy, don't you recognize me?"

My mind struggled desperately to place that smile.

"I'm Seidei!"

Like a light entering a dark room when the door is suddenly thrust open, it all came back to me in an instant!

"Seidei!" I cried, rising, and we embraced lovingly. After she introduced her daughters and I introduced Martha, she told me about her life after leaving our school.

She found a Christian church in London and made her profession of faith. After graduating, she entered one of the colleges to continue her studies and there she met a young African from Ghana, a neighboring country of Nigeria, who was also a Christian. They fell in love, married, and she became Mrs. Yora Foluna. His major was international law, and after graduation they went to Ghana, where he now worked as an attorney for a shipping firm in Accra, the capitol city. She was in Nigeria visiting old friends and had planned to come to Lagos to see me and the school again. What a wonderful reunion for both of us.

I couldn't help but think that despite all his efforts, Mr. Agoyla lost the battle. Not to me. To Jesus!

Some years later, after I retired, got married and was living in Minneapolis, Minn., where my husband worked for a major retailing and wholesaling firm, I received a package with a New York City postmark. I knew no one there. The package contained a lovely plastic plate with a painting of two zebras watering at a river's edge. Information on the back of the plate indicated that it had been made in Accra. Seidei immediately came to mind, but no card or note was included.

About two weeks later, Seidei called from New York to ascertain that I had received the plate. It was her way of reminding me of her home in Ghana. She got my address and telephone number from our Foreign Mission Board in Richmond. Her husband had been appointed as Ghana's representative to the United Nations in New York, where they had lived for almost two years. She had planned to visit me, but they were being called home due to a serious family illness.

Again, we had a great conversation which ended too soon. That was the last time I heard from Seidei. But whenever I look at my plate, or hear the name of Accra or Ghana, her smiling face appears in my mind.

DISCIPLINE

Wanaluna was giving a fine speech at one of our first high-school graduation exercises, and had just begun to thank all her teachers. How proud I was of her! Then I heard the phrase, "Miss Hardy's discipline."

Those three words derailed my train of thought and the rest of her speech passed through my head like an evening breeze until applause brought me back to the moment.

Although the phrase was used in a complimentary way, it started me thinking and questioning long into the night. It had stirred up memories and events of the past, some as far back as my childhood.

My family had always struggled, so much so that both my father and mother worked to make ends meet. At 10, I was given responsibility for the house: the cooking, cleaning and ironing as well as for my younger brother, Harold, and younger sister, Margaret. These responsibilities taught me to discipline my time, if everything was to be accomplished to my parents' satisfaction.

I finished high school in three-and-a-half years and had completed a college semester when I returned to graduate with my class. I also completed the requirements for a BA degree in education in three-and-a-half years, and I was soon teaching school, something I had decided I wanted to do when I was a child. To accomplish these things, I learned to discipline myself consummately.

Teaching in rural county schools, some with pot-bellied stoves and multi-grade levels, also required the utmost in discipline. In that environment, the teacher was also the cook, the nurse, surrogate mother to the young ones and anything and everything else required.

— DISCIPLINE —

Hebron School, Bullitt County, Kentucky, 1936

Yes, I was disciplined because I had had to be.

And it appeared to me that successful people in education, business, the arts, athletics and even our own Baptist leaders were successful, to a great degree, because they were disciplined.

As I examined my faith and beliefs, it was quite obvious that the Christian religion, itself, requires obedience, and obedience requires, among other things, discipline. My very presence on the mission field in Africa was a direct result of the obedience I felt to the Lord, and I had disciplined myself to leave my family and friends, my home and life's work, to be obedient.

Yes, I was a disciplined person. Wanaluna had identified me perfectly. Suddenly I felt the need to fall on my knees and thank God for this discipline, which I did. But while I knelt there praying, other questions came to mind:

Am I over-disciplined? Do I, unnecessarily, impose my own discipline on others?

I couldn't answer those questions immediately, but I did recall that our God is a loving God. Had I administered discipline without love? While I was still on my knees, the realization that our God is also a forgiving God made me feel so much better I was able to close my prayers, crawl into bed and enjoy an excellent night's sleep.

I got up the next day determined not to force my degree of discipline on others, nor would I require that degree of discipline from others. As years passed, this became a constant vigilance, and it wasn't difficult, nor surprising, to learn that I was known as a rather strict disciplinarian by both the students and the teachers on my staff. This had manifested itself during my first term in Nigeria when I had the responsibility, and challenge, of expanding our school to include a secondary level and a high-school level.

My daily work load of additional students, curriculum, massive organizational changes and, of course, educating our students to achieve the required test scores to obtain — and retain — British accreditation soon became a 16- to 18-hours-a-day job. Collapsing, totally exhausted, into bed at 1 or 2 a.m. and rising again at 5 or 6 ready to confidently meet the challenges of a new day became routine.

My closer missionary friends cautioned me to "spread out the work load" or "take it easy." It would usually catch up with me and I'd find myself down with malaria due to a weakened resistance. However, I honestly believe, looking back, that I thrived on it all.

A new missionary teacher, recently appointed by the Board and assigned to our school, keenly tested my discipline. I recall leaving the school one morning and hurrying to the residence building

— DISCIPLINE —

where I was afraid I would find her still in bed, though classes were underway. This was the second day she had done this, and it upset me tremendously, Yes, there she was, still asleep, just like the previous day. Raising the mosquito netting I, not so gently, nudged her shoulder until she opened her eyes and sat up. As I had the previous day, I told her how extremely important it was that we, as teachers, set good examples for the students, and that this always began in the areas of presence and punctuality. While she was still sleeping, one of teachers had to watch both her own and the absent teacher's classroom. It was unfair to the students and to the rest of the school staff.

Perhaps I wasn't as tolerant as I should have been, but this young teacher was always up and ready for her class after that. She later transferred to another post, but on her own initiative. I never reported the incidents.

Had I been too hard on her, I later wondered. Should I have given her more time to adjust to a new environment, new country, new school?

No, I decided. My job was to build this school, and build it in the fastest and most efficient way possible, if we were to attain the accreditation we needed. It was no secret that there were others in Lagos wishing that we'd fail — and some schools already had. I was determined that Reagan Memorial Southern Baptist Girls' School would NOT fail.

Soon, our students ranged in age from six to 17 and, as with most young people, the teen years required the most vigilance and the most guidance and understanding. In many tribes, African girls eagerly anticipate these years. The accepted custom was for a girl to get pregnant early, thereby freeing herself from the "yoke" of parental dominance so she could set up her own family, where she would be "boss."

This kind of thinking prevailed among young African boys, too. Their primary objective was getting a girl pregnant, since that would lead to formation of their own family. This longing for independence is, I suppose, natural for all teen-agers, but such a custom was all wrong.

It was cooler than usual one evening as I stepped out on my verandah to see if the sun had set. It had, and dusk was rapidly settling in. As I turned to go in, I saw something flash out in the courtyard, like a piece of glass or metal. Further squinting revealed one of our students and a young man embracing out under the trees.

Uninvited young men were not permitted inside the compound. I started to call out, thought better of it, and walked down the steps and started towards them. Seeing me, they broke apart, the girl first. As she darted toward the dormitories the boy ran in the opposite direction. Determined not to let him get away, I ran after him. After quite a game of cat and mouse, with him dashing between and behind the trees and buildings, I caught up with him. He offered no resistance, but dropped his head as I ordered him back out into the lighter part of the yard. My first inclination was to call the police, but instead I asked how he had gained entrance. He said the guard had let him in.

He begged to leave. I granted his wish provided he never set foot in our compound again. I had identified the girl — one of our high-school students.

After I locked the gate behind the boy, I found Betty Seats, one of my dearest friends, waiting on my verandah. She had seen part of the incident and pointed out, with amusement, "Cora Ney, I saw you running after that boy and I must say, old girl, that he is much, much too young for you!'

The next day I sacked the watchman and had the girl brought to my office. Although quite penitent, she offered little information about how long this had been going on or how deeply she was involved. I let her stay in school long enough to determine that she was not pregnant, then suspended her when the school term ended. It would not have been good for the school if she had become pregnant while living there. I was relieved.

Yes, I was a disciplined person. But, without my discipline in the school we were striving so hard to build, we would have had nothing.

Several years later, after I had been transferred north to Jos, where I taught at a boys' school, the principal, Bill Cowley, and his family, were scheduled to leave on furlough, but no interim principal had been named. He asked me to substitute for him the year he was gone and I agreed, not wanting their furlough delayed. During his absence, some of the boys broke a couple of rules.

As acting principal, I knew if I overlooked it, others might be inclined to do the same. I suspended the boys and they remained on suspension until Bill returned. I asked myself over and again if I had, indeed, done the correct thing. "If Bill had been here, would he have suspended them?" I repeatedly asked myself.

When Bill returned I told him of the incident, but added, "In my mind, I feel I did the right thing. However, if you feel they should be reinstated now, I won't be offended."

He did reinstate the boys, but only after a probationary period.

After I retired I was always extremely pleased to hear from former students. Several of them referred to the "discipline you brought to our learning experience." This always made me feel that

I had done the right thing, particularly when I received a letter from a former student who, by then, was holding the same position as principal that I had occupied for 18 years. In part, her letter read as follows:

"I have the honour, today, by the special grace of God, to sit in the seat you sat in many, many years ago and made all of us who passed through under your principalship, to become responsible, progressive and honest women. I am speaking the minds of hundreds of other Reaganites who continue to cherish the discipline you taught us. You should be very happy, and content now, that God made, through you, good Christian women who continue to look back and thank you.

(signed, Mrs. Tutuola Dawody)
Yes, I am happy and content.

'TWAS THE DAY!

Longed for, ecstatically anticipated and vehemently demanded — THE DAY was only a few weeks away! How the excitement was building! Each day, it seemed, a giant ocean wave of enthusiasm grew with boundless energy and elation. October 1, 1960. The Day of Independence. The day Nigeria would take it's place beside other nations of the world, was practically at hand.

The ceremonies were planned and the influential list made of dignitaries who would attend — yes, actually visit the NATION of Nigeria! Artists were preparing paintings, murals and flags in honor or the event. Sculptors were forming all kinds of structures — even a 45-foot-high outline of the country — to be unveiled on that glorious day .

Politicians were "politicking" as never before because, previously, any office they held was in conjunction with, and in subjugation to, the British. Now, the prize would be a place in the new government — the Nigerian Republic. Many details had already been worked out, such as British statesmen serving as counselors to the already appointed body of native Nigerians who would serve an interim period of six months to perhaps two or three years,. Then their PEOPLE, through properly-formed, guided and monitored elections, would formulate their own destiny with their own elected officials.

Each day brought a new torrent of speeches, stories and songs aimed at that historic moment when Britain would honor its promise and the umbilical cord of the mother country would be severed.

We missionaries were excited and happy for the Nigerians. There were references by the African press to the American and

French revolutions which established great nations. The British press preferred to refer to the freedom it had granted to such nations as India and Egypt and how these "offspring" countries had handled their new-found liberties. But we missionaries, who had worked so closely with the Africans, probably knew their strengths and weaknesses, their assets and liabilities, even better than the British did.

We also knew, all too well, that the Nigerian people were not ready for what lay ahead. There was unspoken apprehension among us, not for how the new nation would regard us, Christian missionaries, but for how it would handle the new experience of being independent.

In many previous instances, new African republics soon fell into dictatorships and the people found themselves living in far worse conditions than they had experienced under Colonialism. (This, of course, actually happened in the succeeding years in Nigeria.) But freedom must come, and people must suffer its pains as well as its joys.

One bright morning the "crowning" news was received: Queen Elizabeth's official word that she would attend Independence Day ceremonies! Newspaper articles, radio and television (although still very much in its infancy) simply could not praise this forthcoming royal visit enough. A man climbed the flagpole of the British Embassy, which had just been built, and placed the flag of the British Royal Family immediately under the British and Nigerian flags. No, of course he wasn't arrested. He was a hero to the people and the British Lion winked its aristocratic eye.

My position was one of both apprehension and happiness. It was difficult to get caught up in all the exuberant activity. But I could certainly appreciate the exultation of the Nigerians — particularly of our students. We also planned special events and ceremonies to honor the day. Still, I couldn't conjure up the degree of excitement I felt I should, and I felt a bit guilty .

A week or so later, as I was posting some letters, an envelope in my box caught my eye. An embossed crown on the back flap indicated it was from a British office., but I didn't realize that it was the official Crown of the Queen. It was addressed to:

>Miss Cora Ney Hardy, Principal
>Reagan Memorial Girls' School
>P.O. Box #112
>Yaba, Nigeria

Hurriedly, I opened it. The formal invitation inside read as follows:

>THE BRITISH GOVERNMENT
>IS HAPPY TO EXTEND BEST WISHES THAT
>YOU WILL BE ABLE TO BE PRESENT FOR
>A ROYAL RECEPTION AND TEA FOR HER HIGHNESS
>**QUEEN ELIZABETH**
>TO BE HELD IN THE GARDEN OF THE
>BRITISH EMBASSY AT 4:30 P.M. ON THE
>FIRST DAY OF OCTOBER, IN THE YEAR OF OUR LORD
>NINETEEN HUNDRED AND SIXTY

There was no RSVP. A recipient was almost "commanded" to attend and, if necessary, to eliminate any other functions and engagements in order to be present.

Obviously, I had been invited because I was principal of a British-accredited girls' school, not for any particular accomplishment and certainly not for the person I was.

As I drove back to the compound, however, the idea of being invited to and actually attending a reception for the Queen of England began to excite me. Just as the Nigerian people's excitement over becoming a nation had begun as a small quell (sic) and then had mushroomed into a huge storm, the idea of attending a Royal function was having an analogous effect on me. By the time I got home, my heart was beating like a blacksmith's hammer and my mind was racing at a tremendous pace.

I decided not to tell anyone. After all, the invitation could have been a mistake — yes — I was certain that is what had happened. Still, deep down inside, I hoped desperately that it was genuine.

But what if it was? How would I get there? In our Lorrie? Oh, of course not! By taxi? Probably. What would I wear? I had absolutely nothing suitable for a grand event. Would Kingsway (the only good department store in Lagos) have anything suitable? Would I have time to order anything from home, from England, from anywhere else?

"Oh, for pity's sake!" I finally muzzled my wandering mind. "All this carrying on for nothing. It's a mistake. I'll find out about it soon enough."

Soon enough came two or three days later.

I was at my desk when the telephone rang. I waited, knowing that the African student helping me would answer it.

"It's for you, Ma," Yanei said., her eyes wide in amazement. I wondered why.

"Miss Hardy?" a voice asked in quite a formal way.

"Yes it is," I replied.

"This is Colonel Haines of the British Embassy," a seemingly recognizable voice said, and continued after a curt "Ahem!" (clearing his throat), "I believe I've had the pleasure of meeting you previously at one of the educational meetings?"

Now, I seemed to recall him at one of our meetings.

"Of course," I replied.

"Just following up, you see, to make certain you'd received your invitation to the Queen's Reception on the first of October," the voice continued pompously. "You did, I assume? Receive the invitation, that is?"

I said I had and that I would be privileged to be present. Almost as an afterthought, I added, "May I say what an honor it is to be invited. I'm sure it will be something I'll never forget."

"Ahem," he seemed pleased with my comment. "We will be privileged to have you present for this esteemed event. If there is anything we can do or any questions you need to have answered, please do not hesitate to let us know. Oh, by the way, a limousine — I believe that's what you Americans call it don't you?" After a brief pause he continued, "Of course you do. It will call for you at approximately 3:45 that afternoon. Will that be satisfactory?"

"Of course. How considerate. Thank you," I said.

Then I thought, should I or shouldn't I?

"By the way, Colonel Haines, what do you call that kind of automobile that you're sending for me?"

"Eh?" he stammered. "Oh, of course, yes. Well some of us call it a limousine, too, I believe. Ha! Ha! Well, here's looking forward to a glorious day. Good-bye, Miss Hardy."

I turned to find Yanei's big brown eyes still staring at me. I began to realize that I was, indeed, going to the Queen's Reception. Suddenly, I imagined how Cinderella must have felt, and it both frightened and excited me. Now to prepare myself.

The other missionaries were equally excited about my invitation to "rub elbows" with royalty, as were the African teachers. Right away, they wanted to know what I was going to wear.

"Now Cora Ney," Anita Roper said. "You know you have to uphold the reputation of the school and our Mission Board and our country and . . ."

"Please don't go any further," I pleaded, holding up my hands. "I'm already a nervous wreck."

A quick search through my closet and my packed clothes revealed nothing, absolutely nothing suitable. I needed an ankle-length, or at least lower-calf length, party dress. I made a quick trip to Kingsway and found five or six possibilities, but they were sheath-type, very close-fitting or even tight. I did not like that style and it certainly wasn't something a missionary should wear.

I was disappointed and concerned. As I was leaving I spotted a pattern section in a remote part of the store. I shuffled through their dress patterns, mostly from England and France, but I did find some from America, and one in particular interested me. It had no pleats, but it did gather at the waist and was almost ankle-length. I liked it.

But did I have TIME to make it? I found a suitable material in dark blue, my favorite color and one that would fit any occasion. Since there were white contrasting pieces in the design at the waist and imitation pocket tops, I also bought a small piece of off-white material.

Now I needed a hat. I had always loved broad-brimmed hats and had brought a couple with me to Africa. None of the hats at Kingsway came anywhere close to being suitable.

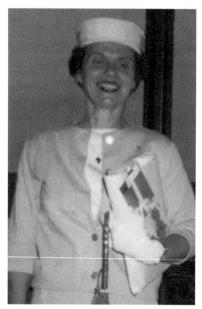
Ready for Queen Elizabeth's reception.

I spent several "early mornings" making the dress and liked it even more when it was finished. But what about a hat? I tried my two broad-brimmed ones, but they were not complimentary to the dress. When I returned them to their boxes I spotted another box containing a small pillbox hat purchased during my last furlough. I took it out and studied it. Amazing! It was the same off-white color as my dress trim. Tucked inside was an open veil in the same color. Would this do?

Time was growing short. I tried on my dress and was extremely pleased. Then I put on the hat, pulling the veil out and down around my face and chin. I decided it would do. Besides, there would be a large crowd at the reception and it probably wouldn't be proper to wear a wide-brimmed hat that might block the view.

Everyone wanted to see the Queen. My pillbox hat would have to do. And I liked it with my dress, especially with the veil.

On Independence Day our students put on a fine program that many of the other Lagos educators attended. We all went to one of the many parades, one held during the noon hour. We did not attend the official ceremonies that formally turned over control of the government from the British to the Nigerians. We knew the crowd would be formidable and key events would be replayed on television.

Precisely at 3:45 p.m., as the Colonel had stated, the limousine arrived at our compound. All the girls and teachers came out to witness it. I gave a short wave in response to the big smiles aimed in my direction as it pulled away. They were enjoying it as much as I was. Another passenger, an Englishman, was also headed for the reception. We also picked up a British Lagos official before reaching the Embassy.

As we passed through the gates, six smartly-dressed guards in brilliant British scarlet with gold tassels snapped to attention. Six more opened the limousine doors and also snapped back to attention. Two others led us into the Embassy where Colonel Haines and the British Ambassador greeted us. The others presented their invitations, but I had not been advised to bring mine and had not. Colonel Haines, sensing my concern, nodded with a smile and introduced me. Then he motioned us on through the long center hall, out into a huge garden at the rear.

The garden's many plants were all elegantly mounted and trimmed. About 200 guests were already present, talking and drinking. A waiter approached with a huge golden tray with different kinds of tea and crumpets (cookies) and I helped myself to both. To one side, under a cluster of trees, the members of a 12-piece band — formally dressed in bright red with black-and-gold trim - were talking with some of the guests.

The Lagos constable and his wife worked their way over to me and we chatted for a moment. The principal of one of the Catholic schools, Father Werrington, also came over to chat. Everything was quite formal and cheerful.

Conversations ended when the band began to play an introduction and those seated immediately arose. Two housemen walked slowly through the guests, creating a six-to-eight-foot opening in the crowd. Everyone looked toward a rose-covered canopy about 20 feet from the hallway through which we had entered the garden. An elderly guardsman, immaculately uniformed and possessing a rather full red mustache and beard, appeared under the canopy after a short drum roll and announced in a loud voice: "Her Majesty, the Queen!"

As he stepped aside the band struck up "God Save the Queen" and everyone turned to face the British flag on a high pole in the garden. Immediately beneath it was the Royal Family flag, but no Nigerian flag at this time.

The Queen appeared under the canopy and the guests chanted, loudly, "LONG LIVE THE QUEEN!" Then a softer repeat, much like an echo, "Long live the Queen!"

With a faint roll of drums, the Queen and her entourage began an extremely slow walk through the opening created by the housemen. Sometimes she paused to speak to a guest, then continued through the crowd, nodding to everyone she could see. Almost everyone in the front row bowed or curtsied, and the Queen nodded in acknowledgment. Then those in front stepped aside so everyone behind them would have a good view of the Queen.

I had a straight-on view of her. I had practiced my curtsy but it still seemed very awkward to me. However, I would do my best. As she came closer I could see guests across from me bowing their heads in addition to nodding and curtsying. When she was within 15 or 20 feet, I saw something which startled me. Now, I didn't know, nor did any of the guests with whom I had spoken know what the Queen would be wearing on her head. Well, she was wearing a pillbox hat. It was much larger than mine and had no veil. But I had to chuckle to myself, because it was white, just like mine!

Careful now, I thought, I can't let my thoughts control my reaction. She was ten feet away, then five. To my left I could see guests bowing and curtsying. Just as I saw her eyes glance towards mine I dropped my head and made my curtsy. It was an experience I shall never forget.

But the best was yet to come. She had barely passed when, suddenly, she made a quick turn of the head and looked back directly at my hat and smiled a quick, soft smile, and just as quickly went on. No one else seemed to notice, but I was thrilled beyond description. I glanced around to see if there were any other pillbox hats. I could see none.

I purchased two sterling-silver napkin holders, each bearing the Queen's engraved crown symbol, so I would always have something to remind me of my "date with royalty." Two were all I could afford, and only because of Christmas money from my family that I'd been holding until the right present came along. This was the right present. It would always remind me of a day very unusual for a missionary to experience.

DR. JOMBO

I threw on my clothes, stepped into my shoes, crammed things into my purse and was hurrying through the front gate when I saw her.

There she was again across the road, stretching to peer into our school compound. This was the third or fourth time I had seen her in a couple of weeks but, because of my usual whirlwind of activity, I had ignored her and hurried on. This time at least, I thought, I'll give her a smile. She didn't see it. Her concentration was centered on what she glimpsed through the gate while it was open. I took a few steps then, well, I don't know — something went off in my head. I slowed down and turned to look at her. She paid no attention, but when I crossed the street to her, she finally looked at me.

She was a skinny, dirty, ugly little girl wearing little more than filthy rags. Her face was expressionless and she didn't move; she just looked at me.

I asked if she would like to come inside. Her eyes widened, but still no response. Taking her little soiled hand, I said, "Come on, if you want to. I'll let you see our school." She didn't resist as I opened the gate and led her inside. She followed me but no longer held my hand. Considering the condition of the girl and her clothes, it was just as well. What if she had some kind of "bug" or disease, that I was bringing right into our habitat!

We visited the classrooms, the chemistry lab, the art room, the cafeteria and dormitories. Her eyes widened for the second time when I showed her one of the blue-and-white uniforms that each student wore. She didn't try to touch it. In fact, she touched nothing, letting me open and close all of the doors, cabinets, etc. Considering her lack of cleanliness, I was somewhat relieved.

Back at the gate, I asked, "Would you like to go to this school someday?"

Yoruba Bush Girls near Shaki, 1955

Her eyes widened again, she took a step backwards and, with a look of terror, exclaimed, "Oh, no! No! I couldn't go to school!"

"Why not?" I asked.

"My father would never let me," she gasped.

Two conflicting thoughts kept exchanging places in my mind:

The first was of the extremely hungry appetite young Nigerians had for education. If possible, they would fight each other for the opportunity to go to school. (Quite the opposite of our American children, many of whom have to be made to attend school.)

The second was of a girl's place in the minds of many Nigerian fathers. They believed a girl was non-educable, and even if she were, she shouldn't be. A girl's place was to grow up, get married, have babies and help her husband work in the fields. This was the expected life for the feminine sex. Our Reagan Memorial School for Girls was but a single drop of sand in the desert as we worked to modify this accepted lifestyle.

But as infinite as it was, we were still making progress.

I put my hand on her shoulder. "Look," I said gently, "if you come by my office once or twice a week during the evening, I'll see what I can do to prepare you to take our entrance tests and we'll see what happens."

Her lack of expression made me wonder if she understood. Then, thinking of her condition and her clothes, I went on:

"Before you come, wash yourself — knees, feet — your entire body. Get yourself as clean as you can and wear the cleanest clothes you have."

Still no expression or response.

I set a date for the following week but really didn't expect to see her again. Perhaps, I thought, it's for the best. I walked back to my office wondering about the hundreds of thousands, perhaps millions, of little girls just like her. How fortunate I was to be born in a land where girls are so privileged. In the good old USA, we take so much for granted.

The days flew by as usual. I had penciled in her name on my calendar, but didn't expect her to come. But, lo and behold, there she was. Her body was clean and her skimpy clothes were clean but full of holes. She was right on time, and her punctuality encouraged me.

Those first evenings were challenging for us both and a bit disheartening to me. She possessed absolutely no comprehension. But for her stick-to-it-iveness I would have stopped the sessions.

After several weeks the "counting" process began to penetrate Jombo's little head and her "letters" were improving. I felt she was ready to test, but dare I follow through? I knew nothing about her or her family. But her indomitable effort had won my full support — and my heart. I discussed Jombo with my staff and we decided to let her take the tests.

Six or eight girls took the qualification tests, but my mind was only on Jombo — and I could hardly wait to learn the results. I was tempted to sit in on the grading but thought better of it. She passed.

Now other problems loomed ahead. Permission from her family and, if they couldn't or wouldn't pay, who would?

I asked her to bring her father to see me. This perturbed her, but she did. He was quite ill at ease despite all I could do to make him feel welcome. He was unusually tall and thin, with a slight bend in his back. He, his father and his grandfather had all been farmers, and Jombo was destined to work in the fields. When I told him what we had been doing and that she did well on our initial tests, he didn't seem impressed. After several minutes of apathetic conversation, it was obvious that he wouldn't mind her going to school, but there was no way he or his family would pay. When our meeting ended he seemed relieved to go, taking his little daughter with her suddenly-acquired knowledge with him. She looked back at me with no expression.

But I was determined that all those evenings weren't going to waste — for either of us. No funds were available within our operating budget, so I decided to pray about it, leaving it up to the Lord to tell me what to do. I went to bed and the solution came to me in about 15 minutes. My brother Harold always sent a generous check at Christmas and a note indicating that it was "for you, your personal needs. It is not intended to be a subsidy for the Mission Board or your school." My wonderful brother with the flame-red hair and face full of freckles. You see, I always remembered him as the little brother I cared for when I was in charge of our home while Mother and Dad worked.

I always used some of his yearly gift personally, stopping by Rome, Switzerland, Vienna, etc., on my trips home — seeing places I otherwise would never see. I was always with another homecoming missionary or missionary couple. And I always wanted to get home as quickly as possible, so one or two days was all I'd spare.

So part of Harold's gift would pay little Jombo's way to Reagan Memorial School. In addition, I was sponsored in Nigeria by the Campbellsville Baptist Church in Campbellsville, Ky., and a couple of church members frequently sent me some monies. I always arranged to speak to this wonderful church and its faithful members more than once during each furlough. Oh, how happy they were when I went there to speak — the church's pews would be filled.

So with those monies and part of Harold's gift, Jombo would get her chance! Its amazing how the Lord works things out — when we let Him.

Jombo, after an unusually slow beginning that required special tutoring, became an excellent student. How proud I was of her and I could tell she knew it! Her face began to show emotion and betray her thoughts.

When I was transferred north to Jos, my personal contact with her ended. She was in high school by then and I made certain the school continued to receive funds for her to graduate.

A few years later, I was delighted to learn from one of her teachers visiting in Jos that Jombo was studying at a university in London on a scholarship.

Later on, I heard she did extremely well at the university and had enrolled at a school of medicine, again on scholarship. How I longed to see her and give her a pat on the back! Later on, I heard she had returned to Nigeria to practice medicine, but our paths never again crossed — in Nigeria.

Years later, after my husband retired and we had returned to our beloved Kentucky, we finally made contact. Jombo telephoned from Nigeria to say she was coming to the United States and had routed herself through our home town, Florence, Ky., and was anxious to see me again. Oh, how this thrilled me, and when I shared my joy with Roy, he could see what it meant to me.

We met her at the airport, and when this beautiful, extremely well-groomed and impeccably-dressed woman came up and put her arms around me, I didn't know her. She far surpassed what I had imagined she would be like. Her use of the English language was just as impeccable, and we chatted unceasingly on the way to our home.

"I've met several of your African friends," Roy remarked later, "but this lady is the most impressive one of all!"

"Well," I replied, "you should have seen how she looked when I first saw her," and I told him her complete story.

Is there any place special you'd like to see or visit in Kentucky?" Roy asked her. "Oh," Jombo said, "I've seen pictures of those gorgeous animals in beautiful green fields, all enclosed in pretty white fences. How far away are those?" A trip to Lexington and the bluegrass region, about an hour away, was quickly planned for the next day.

As we began a buffet dinner we had put together before picking Jombo up at the airport, she handed a folded piece of paper to me. It explained why she was in the States. She was headed for Durham, N.C., to receive an honorary degree from the Duke University Medical School for her "efforts in the field of abdominal surgery, working with her own native Nigerian people!"

I was too stunned to say anything, but extremely pleased and proud. She asked me to join her at the ceremony. I was so happy and surprised that it took me a few moments to decide. But there was only one possible answer — I had to decline. I explained that I had only 5-10% vision due to macular degeneration of the retina. She made an attempt to change my mind, but seemed to understand that I would be "only in the way," as I put it. Her disappointment was almost equal to mine. What I would have given to be there with her and witness that moment. She wrote me about it, with all the details and mentioned a humanitarian from Scotland and a doctor from Finland who received honorary degrees along with her.

Our trip through the bluegrass section was wonderful, her enjoyment only surpassed by ours.

"Just like the pictures I've seen," she remarked again and again.

Jombo picked up on horse lingo — foal, mare, filly, etc. — and used the words in absolute correctness. I recalled what a difficult time she had preparing for her entrance tests at Reagan Memorial, but now, how quickly she learned! "What a prodigious journey her life has made," I thought, "and who knows what still lies ahead for her?"

Driving through Lexington, we passed the Albert B. Chandler Medical School and we explained that it was the University of Kentucky's School of Medicine.

"Why, that's where (Dr.) Roger Combs teaches and practices," she said. "You see," — it was as if she'd suddenly discovered familiar ground — "he comes out every other year, entirely on his own — paying his own expenses and never charging a nira (Nigerian money). He helps so very much, examining children and the elderly and prescribing treatment and medicine. We look forward to his trips so very much. So that's where he works!"

Then she added a phrase, and I knew Roy must be splitting his insides silently laughing about it, and I was too, but we didn't show our reactions in any way. She said, matter-of-factly, revealing it certainly wasn't the first time she had used the phrase nor, in all probability would it be the last: "He's a pain-in-the-ass about details. But I guess its better to be that way than the opposite. He does keep us in line with what we should be doing, too."

The next morning we put her on the plane for Durham. She looked back and waved, smiling at us. As we left I thought of all the work she and I had experienced and the miraculously long way she had come. Sometimes, the Lord lets us see the results of our labors. Not often, of course, but when He does, they are always incredible!

Oh yes, she also had been teaching a Sunday-school class in the Christian church she regularly attends in Ibadan.

"CASING THE JOINT"

Have you ever tried to complete a final draft of an important plan, document or program and, because of interruptions or distractions, felt you were making no progress?

That's how I felt one morning at school. My plan had to be turned in to the Board late that day, so I decided to go home, where interruptions would be minimal. Gathering my materials, I left word that I'd return by early afternoon. At home, in my haste to get to work, I neglected to lock the front gate, but did lock my residence door. Soon, inundated with facts and figures, I felt confident I could finish the project on time.

Suddenly, there was a knock at my door. Leaving everything spread out on my table, I went to the door. A young man in a dress suit, white shirt and tie was standing outside.

Please, Ma," he said graciously, "would you mind, terribly, if I used your water closet? I need to do so in the worst way."

Having been in a similar situation several times, and considering how well-dressed and polite he was, I was tempted, but not totally convinced to let him in.

"I'm Mioga, a student at your Boys' High School across town,' he said. And, sizing him up, it seemed that I had even seen him there. Feeling he was someone I could trust, and anxious to get back to my project, I let him in. I pointed out the water closet and he went straight to it. I returned to my work in the next room and got so involved I forgot he was in my house.

I had put down my pencil and was looking out over the room, completely caught up in my thoughts when I caught a glimpse of the young man in a mirror across the room. I was so startled I almost cried out. He had a small pad of paper and a pencil and, as he glanced around, he was taking notes. I knew exactly what he was doing. He was a THIEF taking inventory for a future trip back to rob me.

Thieves were thick in Nigeria then and anyone with possessions had to maintain constant vigilance. Nigeria was Africa's most populated country and many of its "have-not" inhabitants had no way to gain an education or better themselves. So thievery flourished. Despite arrests and convictions, it remained the country's major criminal activity and was increasing at an alarming rate. The have-nots thought nothing of obtaining the material things they could never hope to have honestly, through thievery.

When I walked down a street, went to the city or took a trip into the countryside or the Bush, my heart swelled with compassion for the poverty that was so evident. Ironically, Nigeria has so much potential, with it's wealth of oil, mineral deposits of coal, tin and columbite along with agricultural potential and other valuable resources.

But until recently, the Nigerians' inability to mine the minerals, remove the oil from the ground or capture the value of all its resources has kept Nigeria a relatively poor, undeveloped nation. Thus the high rate of poverty.

As I watched that young man take notes I became quite alarmed. If I approached him, would he become agitated and harm me? If I waited until he let me know he was ready to leave, would he return later to rob me? What other choices were there? My telephone was on a stand halfway between my work table and the water closet. Grasping a pair of scissors and a granite paperweight, I tiptoed over to it, keeping an eye on the doorway from my room to the hall and the water closet. The realization that he could come round that corner at any time sent shivers up and down my spine.

I dialed the operator and asked for the police in one breath. He had to have heard me.

"One moment, please," I responded to an officer's "Hello".

Raising my voice, I stated clearly, "You are NOT one of our students. I don't know who you are but I know what you're doing!"

There was no response. I went on, "I have the police on the telephone. They're only a block away and can be here in five minutes. All I have to do is tell them to come." I paused, but there was still no response or movement. So I went on, "Now, if you drop that pad and pencil on the floor — right where you are — and get out of this house," I paused to catch my breath, "I won't tell them to come and you will not be caught and prosecuted."

Again there was silence. "Will you GET OUT OF HERE!" I yelled, "or do you want to be arrested?"

There was a sudden streak of movement as he dashed past my doorway. He paused to open the outside door, then ran off the verandah and into the yard. I told the policeman I had just encountered a thief in my house, but he ran into the yard and was gone. He said he would send someone over right away.

I hurried to the door and saw the would-be thief flash through the iron gate into the street. I locked the door and went to the water closet, where I found his pad and pencil on the floor. Within minutes the police arrived, took the pad and pencil and questioned me. I received a polite but thorough "thrashing" from them, which I deserved.

"Miss Hardy," they both admonished, "NEVER, ever let anyone you don't know into your house again." They didn't have to worry. I had certainly learned my lesson.

I was far too excited to return to my project and just had to thank the Lord I had not been harmed. It taught me another lesson I never forgot: Regardless of how difficult a project is or how urgently it needs to be finished, always maintain a keen sense of security.

Miss Hardy's 50th birthday.

MEMORABLE MEALS

In 30 years, there were so many wonderful get-togethers and meals, it's impossible to recall them all, though each was a joy unto itself. Large, small, formal, family-style and eat-and-run meals, we experienced them all.

I can still hear dear Vivien Nowell's marvelous voice. After a meal was ready, the table set, and we had thanked the Lord for our blessings — just before the first fork, spoon or knife touched food — her voice would peacefully ascend: "Now let's all just take our time and enjoy it!"

All my life I have loved to entertain, and especially in Africa, for I liked meeting new people — missionaries as well as others — and whether it was a meal, tea time, or a round of conversation, it was my moment of living life to its fullest. This was particularly true in Lagos. Because of its major port of entry and business and cultural hub, opportunities were ever present: Greeting incoming missionaries and their families, saying good-bye to those leaving on furlough, meeting and getting to know some of the American and English business people and their families. We all had something in common, being away from home. All of this and more, much more, provided me with the chance to play hostess. I never let an occasion go by. But my purse strings were often stretched to the breaking point. I wouldn't have had it any other way.

When our top five girls got the highest British Scholarship grades of all the contestants in western Africa, we were so proud of them we thought something very special should be done. Our school wanted to show how much we appreciated the long, difficult hours they had spent preparing for the tests. Their test results helped put our school "on the map," so to speak. We decided to let the girls choose what they'd like to do.

They were surprised and pleased, and almost in unison gave the same answer. "What is that feast you have every year where you take out of your food closets some of the things you've brought back from home? You take all day preparing it and so many of you gather together for it, it always seems to be a wonderful and tasty feast!"

We looked at each other, mildly amazed. We had had no idea that our Thanksgiving Day dinners made such an impression on the girls.

"You mean a Thanksgiving Day dinner?" a teacher asked.

"Yes, that's it," they responded. "Isn't that your American feast day?"

We told them it was a kind of feast day, but more than anything else, it was a day of giving thanks to God for his goodness to us throughout the year. And although we thanked him every day in our prayers, this was one special day we set aside to thank him as a nation. We told them how Pilgrims started it back in the 1600s and invited American Indians to participate and that Thanksgiving had become a national holiday all Americans looked forward to every year.

"But the food!"' they exclaimed. "You seem to go to such time and effort in getting it ready. It must be delicious!"

We felt a little ashamed that we had failed to convey the "why" of the holiday.

"Please," they continued, "we'd like to have a feast like that one." Then they added, "But only if it's alright."

"Of course it's alright," we said, and set a date and time. The girls were tremendously excited and word spread quickly throughout the school. They were already regarded as something special by the other students, but this placed them on an even higher plane —

having an American Thanksgiving Day dinner! In their minds, there could be no higher honor.

The day arrived and we started the dinner, quickly realizing what made the meal stand out in the students' minds. The cook usually handled meal preparations, but on a few days each year we took over the kitchen and made the dinners, and Thanksgiving was one of those days. Little wonder they thought it extraordinary.

We put the turkey in the oven, opened cans of cranberry sauce, olives, mushrooms and peas, most of which we had brought from back home, prepared the dressing, and made Waldorf salad and pumpkin pie.

We decided to serve a pre-meal cocktail of tomato juice. We always added a squirt or two of lemon juice to add zip to the taste.

We were finally ready and sent for the girls, who were waiting in anxious anticipation.

First we had the cocktails, then sat down in the dining room, with the girl who attained the highest test score at the head of the table as a place of honor. We said a Thanksgiving-Day blessing and began the meal.

The girls had difficulty with everything but the turkey. There were no calls for second helping, despite our urging.

"Oh, its good," or "Well, its a little different from what I expected," or "Yes, I like it," they'd say when we asked about various dishes. But it was obvious they were not enjoying the meal, not even that pumpkin pie which we thought would be the crowning point of the meal.

So, instead of discussing the food, we talked with them about their homes and families and answered questions about ours. They never seemed to hear enough about our families.

Several days later we had the same five girls together and, seizing the moment, I asked Kiahzi, the eldest, what had gone wrong with the Thanksgiving dinner. She insisted everything had been good. The others quickly echoed her favorable comments.

"Look," I said, staring each of them, in turn, in the eye, "when you ate so little and took each and every bite in a slow and deliberate manner, well, we teachers aren't dumb - - you know that — we could tell you didn't care for the food." They looked at each other, trying to decide if it would be acceptable to tell how they really felt. Individually at first, then totally in concert, they told how each of the foods tasted — to them.

We should have known; they were accustomed to a completely different taste. Hadn't we been aware of our cook's meals, how they were seasoned, their consistency and how they were served? None of us cared for many of these dishes either. It should have been obvious what their response would be to an American cooked and seasoned meal.

"But," one of our teachers said, "they wanted an American Thanksgiving dinner and that's what we gave them."

Of course, that's exactly what happened. I'll never forget how, once the silence was broken, each girl identified what she considered the worst-tasting item: the peas, the dressing, the salad. Although they enjoyed the turkey, they preferred a less-seasoned fowl, the way our cook always prepared it.

During this eye-opening session, one of the girls popped out with, "Please, Ma, what was that red stuff?"

"You mean the cranberry sauce we served," I asked.

"Oh no, not that," she said, and all the others joined in with: "That red stuff we drank before we sat down to eat."

"Oh," I said, "you mean the tomato juice."

"Is THAT what it was?" they asked, looking dubiously at each other.

I nodded. "That's what it was. Now I know you all like tomatoes, you have them frequently."

"Well,' they said, "that was the very WORST OF ALL!"

Apparently that little squirt of lemon juice didn't taste so zippy to them.

On another occasion, I was looking forward to a Saturday evening meal with Percy Wilhyte, a vice president with Barclays' Bank in England, his wife, and two Americans, John Sturgeon and his wife. Shell Oil exported a considerable amount of oil from Nigeria and John headed up their Nigerian office. Both couples had expressed a craving for a good American dinner. All the English folks we knew thought American foods far superior to English.

Our regular cook was off that Saturday and I almost asked for a postponement. However, Josiah assured me he could obtain the services of a very fine African cook to fill in. When the cook was introduced to me at noon that Saturday, I noticed he was, bluntly put, very fat, with a huge stomach.

I asked if he knew how to prepare American hamburgers. He smiled, revealing several gold teeth, and nodded. Josiah interpreted, saying he had prepared them before. The cook put his hands together to illustrate how he patted the meat to form patties.

Evening soon arrived, along with the two couples. While they sat sipping zippy tomato-juice cocktails, I decided to take a quick tour of the kitchen to check on the cook. I had told my guests we were having American hamburgers as our main dish, news they received with a hearty cheer.

As I neared the kitchen I heard humming and singing. "He obviously enjoys cooking," I said to myself, opening the door. Then I stopped and stared in horror! There he was, shirt off, sitting on a stool and leaning slightly backwards, with six or seven raw hamburger patties on his rotund belly. He would pick them up, pat them between his hands, then, as he laid them back on his stomach, he patted them against his perspiring skin again, singing all the while.

My first thought was to stop his unsavory actions and order him off the grounds. But upset as I was with the cook, I was even more upset with Josiah for bringing him into my kitchen. I headed for Josiah's room. He saw me coming and knew from my expression that I was terribly upset. I yelled, "Get that man out of here this instant. Do you hear me, get him out!"

Without answering, he headed for the kitchen and, in a minute or two, he had dispatched the cook and joined me in the kitchen. I did not dare use those patties. I had no idea what kind of bacteria might be in them and though grilling might kill the germs, just the thought of where the patties had been almost made me vomit.

"And to think," I said to myself, "I went to great effort to get that beef and ground it up, personally. " I decided to substitute some chicken our regular cook had cut up before he left that morning. I told Josiah, who was now ready to jump through hoops to please me, to get it out of the fridge. (Refrigerator to Americans.) Fortunately, the quantity was adequate. Josiah began mixing the batter and I returned to my guests and told them there had been a slight delay.

As I started back to the kitchen, I said, "I'm very sorry to tell you that instead of hamburgers we're having a rare American delicacy — Southern," I hesitated and corrected myself, "KENTUCKY fried chicken!"

They applauded and said gleefully, "that's even better. H-m-m! H-m-m!"

This was before Colonel Harlan Sanders' Kentucky Fried Chicken became so widely known back in the States. Whenever I told this story after he became a national household name, I claimed that it was I who came up with that name, "KENTUCKY FRIED CHICKEN."

Everyone raved about the chicken and we had a wonderful time. I understand Kentucky Fried Chicken has expanded into several foreign countries, including England. I often wonder if the Wilhytes, who ate many pieces that evening, ever associate my fried chicken with the famous Colonel Sanders' recipe?

My good friend Audrey Cowley and her husband, Bill, decided to give a birthday party in my honor. Audrey was very busy at the time. Besides raising two young girls and keeping house, she helped her husband and others in the mission field wherever and whenever possible. But she just had to have a dinner party for my birthday.

I arrived early, in case I could help. She was hurrying this way and that, her hair not yet fixed, getting the final items ready for the meal. She proudly showed me the beautiful birthday cake she had baked. I was surprised and very pleased. I couldn't recall ever having a formal birthday dinner party before, and I liked it.

There wasn't time for dessert after the meal because of a program at the Hillcrest MK (Missionary Kids) School we all wanted to see. We decided to leave the cake for later. Audrey set it on a counter where she was sure it was high enough to be safe from Champ, their well-disciplined dog.

After the program, Bill and Audrey invited several others to share a piece of the cake, making a much larger party than originally planned. Fortunately, we got back to the house before the others to find that Champ had, indeed, taken a bite out of the cake.

"Get out of here, Champ," Audrey screamed. "Get out of here before I . . . . Oh, mercy, now what am I going to do?"

There sat that beautiful chocolate-iced cake with a huge corner missing.

"It's too late to bake another one. They'll be here any minute," she wailed. "Oh, what are we going to do?"

My heart went out to her. She had worked so hard to have this happen at the last minute.

"That's all right, just a part of the cake was touched," I tried to console her.

"Nobody wants to eat a cake a dog has nibbled on," she replied, almost in tears.

I picked up a knife and cut off the damaged corner. "He only touched this part," I pointed out. "No one will ever know what happened. And there's absolutely no reason we should tell them."

"Do you really think not? she questioned.

"Of course not," I replied. "Now go on and get things ready. If anyone arrives, I'll greet them."

She left with a look on her face that betrayed her doubts. But not one person questioned the missing corner; perhaps they never noticed. And everyone raved about how good it tasted. And indeed it did!

As Audrey and I caught each other's eye across the room we knew we had a secret that would bind us even closer, if possible.

Perhaps my biggest cooking challenge came after I was transferred from Lagos to Jos. Lagos was a bustling bundle of energy, Jos a comparatively small, semi-rural, quieter community. So, of course, my opportunities for entertaining were substantially diminished.

But Hillcrest, our MK school, was located nearby. It was necessary for the missionaries' children to have a separate school; they needed a different curriculum if they were to continue their education in American colleges, which many did.

When I was on furlough in 1958, Bill and Audrey visited me while I was staying with my sister's family. My sister's children called me Auntie (with the broad "A" sound), and afterwards Bill and Audrey's children called me Auntie too. Soon all the MKs were doing so. It made me feel closer to them, and to home.

The MKs liked to come to my house for snacks of popcorn, fudge, cookies and, best of all, my waffles. I brought waffle irons back from a trip home, and brought back yet another set on a subsequent trip, I experimented with several varieties: Belgian, Scottish, etc. The children loved them all and I loved making waffles for them.

I visited Hillcrest for a program one day, and afterwards the children gobbled down a couple of pizzas someone had brought. "If they are this crazy about pizza," I thought, "I've got to try a piece," and I did. I had never liked Italian food or any dish containing tomato sauce and I found pizza to be, well, just so-so. But if the kids loved it that much, I had to learn to make it. But I wouldn't dare ask.

I hoped to take a couple of stabs at making pizza before their next visit, because I heard a couple of kids say "I bet Auntie makes great pizza — everything else she makes is go good!"

Two nights before their visit I tried to recall what was in a pizza. The base was a crust, not too thick. then there was a meat, either ground beef, pork or something similar, and shredded cheese, olives and, if I recalled correctly, mushrooms.

— MEMORABLE MEALS —

These are wonderful, tasty ingredients, I thought. But then they ruin it all by covering it with that horrible tomato sauce.

First, the dough. I used flour and water, as if I were making biscuits, but rolled it extremely thin with baking powder and just a bit of yeast, realizing that it would rise when it got hot. Next came the beef, which I ground myself, seasoned with onion, garlic powder and cayenne pepper and sautéed in a skillet. Next came the cheese. All I had was Jack cheese, so it would have to do. I shredded it thickly.

Then I opened cans of mushrooms and olives and a can of tomato sauce, mixed it with the same seasoning I used in the meat and added catsup, which made it bulkier. I spread the dough out on a baking sheet and slowly added the other ingredients, finishing with tomato sauce and cheese, with mushrooms and olives on top, and put it in the oven.

"What on earth do you think you're doing, Cora Ney?" I said to myself, "trying to make something, all by yourself, that you've never made before and that you don't like to eat." I tried two or three times, and each pizza tasted worse than the previous one to me.

After school was dismissed on Friday, I hurried home to produce a final version. After I put it in the oven, I prayed very hard, in silence.

Well, it came out of the oven smelling and even looking like the one I had seen the children eating. Some slight revisions in the amount of seasoning, preparatory work and baking time from my first trials appeared to have paid off.

I was starting a second pizza when they hit my front door, excited and hungry and about two hours earlier than expected. But when one of them yelled that the rehearsal for the Gilbert & Sullivan operetta was canceled, it explained everything.

"Well, I said, "one's already done and there on the table. Why don't you cut it and help yourselves? They did, gulping it down with shouts of "Um-m-m" and "Oh-h-h". I was so relieved that, in a corner where I couldn't be seen, I said a little "thank you" to God.

Soon after, whenever I passed a group of the children, I began hearing the phrase, "Auntie makes the best pizza.!"

"Auntie makes the best everything!" another voice would respond.

There is one memorable dish I cannot leave out of my recollection. Whether it reached us through a relocated missionary couple who had served in India or a British couple who had lived there several years, is uncertain. But groundnut stew was relished by so many missionaries that I had to include it here. After retirement, I was often called upon by my church, during missions weeks, to prepare this dish for the missions banquet. It met the criteria for a foreign meal and always went over in grand style. It requires no side dishes.

WEST AFRICAN GROUNDNUT STEW

1 chicken (4-5 lbs., cut up)	ADDED CONDIMENTS
2 packages onion soup mix	grated carrots, diced celery,
1/2 tsp. pepper	onions, tomatoes, cucumbers,
2 tsp. red chili powder	green peppers, apples,
1 cup chopped celery	orange & grapefruit sections,
1 6-oz. can tomato paste	sieved hard-boiled eggs,
6 cups water	groundnuts*, bananas,
1/2 cup flour	toasted & plain coconut, raisins,
1 cup peanut butter	cubed pineapple (fresh if possible)
3 tbsp curry powder	fried crisp bacon & okra
	Spanish or cocktail nuts will do

Combine ingredients in a large pot and heat to boiling. Reduce heat and simmer two or three hours until chicken is tender. Remove chicken and debone it. Combine 1/2 cup sifted flour with 1/2 to 3/4 cup water to make a smooth paste. Add it to the broth with one cup of peanut butter (smooth or chunky) and 3 tablespoons of curry powder, mixed with water.

Put condiments in serving bowls. Diners choose their condiments, then add broth and chicken. Condiments may also be served with rice, if desired, as side dishes.

STRESSFUL CHANGE

I had worked for and looked forward to the day the Reagan Memorial principalship would be turned over to a Nigerian. But in my mind this eventful day was off somewhere in the future. However, when I thought it over after it happened, it was quite obvious that the day should have come even sooner than it did.

I learned with chagrin that the Board didn't quite know how to approach me about it. Perhaps they thought I would initiate the action. But I was so busy and so intent on continuing the school's progress that it never occurred to me. There were always "projects" which took the majority of my time, efforts and thoughts.

Mrs. Adegbite came up through our school and had returned to teach and hold additional responsible positions there. She was to be my replacement. Unnoticed by me, she had made it very clear to others that she felt ready and capable of handling the job.

Wonderful, wonderful Dr. Goerner, who had been my missions professor at the seminary and had, for some time, held the position of Secretary for Africa, Europe and the Near East for our convention, was visiting us. The territory had become so large and unmanageable that, in 1964, Europe and the Near East were consigned to someone else, which left Dr. Goerner with only Africa and enabled him to make trips there more frequently and become more deeply involved.

During this visit, he asked to meet with me. I was always delighted to talk with him because I always came away more knowledgeable and motivated. He began by laughingly referring to my arrival in Nigeria: "Cora Ney, do you remember those first two weeks you were here, how you thought you'd come over just to

The teaching staff at Reagan Memorial School.

teach and ended up not only with the principalship but the heavy load of expanding the school dumped on your shoulders?"

I smiled. "How could I ever forget it?"

'That was about the most inequitable experience that any of our missionaries ever encountered during their very first days in the field," he said, shaking his head.

Then he began to list all the progress made in the school and its recognition as one of the best. Slowly and deliberately he moved to some of the specific achievements and changes: the new lab and lab equipment, and, years later, the new library, all made possible by the Lottie Moon Christmas Offerings. He named several of the curriculum changes and again brought up our high ratings. As we talked, it began to dawn on me what he was doing. I can't describe the feeling I had as that moment of realization engulfed me. There are no words to describe it.

Dr. Goerner was always extremely sensitive to people's feelings. However, the rest of the conversation was very difficult for us both. I realized that this matter should never have reached this point. I had failed to keep foremost in my mind that our basic goal, in the school and elsewhere, was to teach, train and prepare Nigerians for the day they could take on the responsibility of their own people.

I never felt so dreadful in my life.

And I wasn't completely absorbing what he was saying. As I struggled to bring my attention back to him, he said he would like me to transfer north to Jos to teach, and how much better the climate would be for me there. Living practically on the equator in Lagos for as long as l had, with the malaria, the insects and the vibrant heat — well, this was not good for a Caucasian. "Oh," he added, "I don't want you to think we want to turn you out to pasture. Far, far from it." He said that numerous challenges in Jos would keep me busy.

As I listened, my mind drifted back through 18 years of difficulty, progression and fulfillment. I was 33 when I assumed this responsibility and now I was nearing 50. I would be leaving the best years of my life behind — years of toil and tears — but also lots of fulfillment and joy.

Dr. Goerner patted me on the shoulder. "You're a good soldier," he said. "I really and truly wish I had more like you." He left the room and I sat there silently for several minutes, stunned.

As I headed home that evening somehow — I have never been able to explain it — for the first time in my life I felt betrayed. I didn't want to give up my position. I didn't want to go north to Jos. I began to make up reasons about how I had been betrayed. They hadn't even consulted me. Hadn't provided any warning.

I wanted to cry out: "It isn't fair!"

That night found me down on my knees wrestling with my feelings and crying out for God's guidance and counsel. I know not how long I stayed there, alternately praying and laying my weary head

STRESSFUL CHANGE

over on the bed and resting. I knew God hardly ever answered prayers immediately. But slowly, over several hours, a light began to flash off and on in the back of my head — very dimly at first, then brighter and brighter. I saw just how selfish and inconsiderate I had been feeling. It also came to me that I, not Dr. Goerner, not the Board, but I, I should have been at the forefront, initiating a plan for turning over the reins.

I asked forgiveness for my failure and for acting so childishly when I heard the news of my transfer. By 3 or 4 a.m., a quiet peace descended on me. I crawled into bed for a couple of hours of deep sleep before morning

The following weeks were busy with preparations for the transfer of authority. Everything went off smoothly, without incident. At a farewell dinner the entire school — staff and students in turn — presented me with speeches, plaques and remembrances. It was so very thoughtful and considerate and I truly appreciated it. However, although I was at peace with myself over the change, everything was difficult for me, not to accept, but to experience.

Finally, through His leadership and through the words from that same hymn that had brought me to Africa in the first place — "Wherever He Leads, I'll Go" — I began to look northward to my new assignment, it's challenges and new people and environment.

On the day I left, I couldn't help thinking about how our own country's forebears had left their native countries — and perhaps the best years of their lives — to travel across the sea and bring forth our great nation. I thought of our American settlers who braved so many dangers in settling the West, not looking back but moving ever onward. I, too, was determined not to look back, but forward to the new challenges ahead.

THE TWO R'S: R & R

To infer that my time in Nigeria was all grind with little repose would not only be fallacious but outright mendacious. We had numerous times set aside for rest and recreation. However, as far as my own "R & R" was concerned, a letter from home was the best antidote for overwork and a panacea for my yearnings and longings.

In Lagos, I loved to visit Kingsway, and visiting missionaries also found outings there a treat. The department store reminded us of our earlier days and, through clothing styles and decor, kept us somewhat up-to-date on changing tastes in the outside world. Besides, it was the only place in Lagos, or possibly Nigeria, that was AIR-CONDITIONED. Just stepping inside the store brought back memories of shopping at home. Often I couldn't find exactly what I wanted, but Kingsway nonetheless provided escapism.

Not far from Kingsway, still in downtown Lagos was the best restaurant, a Chinese restaurant, and when we missionaries had either saved enough money to afford a meal there or received a personal check from home, it offered a wonderful escape from our daily work load. I'd never favored Oriental food before coming to Nigeria, but I liked most of the dishes they served. And oh, those fortune cookies! We'd laugh and laugh, how much depending on how ridiculous our fortunes turned out to be. One said I was going to have "not one, but two handsome husbands and many children." Another told me that I would "travel several thousand miles from home to engage in my life's work." The ridiculous and reality, all in fortune cookies.

We also spent time at several beaches, occasionally taking along a picnic lunch or supper. A supper was ideal, for we watched the

Cora Ney with her watchdog, Duchess, at her house in Jos.

beautiful African sunset out over the Atlantic Ocean while we ate. We all knew that as that big red ball sank slowly down over the ocean, on the other side lay America and home, friends and family. I never dwelt long on that thought lest feelings I could not easily absorb arise within me.

The beach had its own set of problems. The sand flies were plentiful and simply terrible. Their bites could cause huge skin rashes, and they and other insects always seemed to find ways into one's clothing and belongings. Because we were so close to the equator, we had to be vigilant about getting too much sun. And while the ocean felt refreshing, the salt water clung to our skin like a thick, unwelcome lotion. A bath was always in order after a trip to the beach.

In 1952 or '53 Betty Seats, Ollie Freeman and I and another two or three women went to the beach. Betty strolled along the shoreline, picking things out of the debris that had washed up. She disappeared around a cove that came right down to the shore. But she soon came back, definitely in a hurry, took me aside, and whispered, "Cora Ney, you wouldn't believe what I just saw!"

Betty loved to "cut-up" and have fun, so I laughed and asked if a whale had washed up on shore.

"No," she said, " seriously, "but you might call it a 'whale of a sight!'"

I still thought she was cooking up mischief until she took my hand and led me towards the cove. As we rounded it, three people came into view about a hundreds yards away. I looked at her as if to ask, "Well, what's so unusual about that?," when a second look alerted me. A man and two women were cavorting on the beach completely, totally in the nude! I blinked my eyes and took another look. Then we looked at each other in disbelief. "I've heard of nudists, back in the States," I said, "but I never expected to see them."

Now, such a scene was not shocking, because in Nigeria one learned to expect almost anything at any time. Occasionally, when I was driving through the countryside, I would see an African man urinating, imperturbably, by the side of the road. And bare-breasted African women became more visible as we went further into the country's interior. But the cavorters Betty had stumbled upon were Caucasian and, while it didn't shock us, it certainly surprised us.

We walked back to our friends, wondering if we should tell them. If we did, someone might want to confirm our report. If we didn't, one of them might stumble onto the same scenario.

We decided to say nothing and keep a sharp lookout. Should the unclothed parties venture into our area, there would be time enough to alert the others and pack up and leave.

All evening both Betty and I kept a vigilant eye peeled toward the cove. But no one appeared, at least not until we had finished supper and left, a bit early on this particular night, which drew mild criticism from the others. Back at the school, we told the other ladies why. They laughed and shook their heads, and irrepressible Betty muttered, "Well, I just wish they had come along. I'd have picked up a rock and hit the bull's-eye. That's what I'd have done!" End of story.

Probably my most frequent R & R, at least from 1947 to 1957, was trips to the cinema, or the "films" as our British friends put it. It reminded me a lot of our drive-in movies at home, except there weren't so many automobiles, and there were many, many seats, all outdoors. Most of the movies were British, but occasionally we got an American production. One of the British actors we liked was John Mills, who had the same name as a missionary from Texas. We kidded him about it ("We're going to see John on the movie screen, tonight," etc.) but he gave us back just as much teasing as we handed out.

These British movies heightened my awareness of and appreciation for background music. The credits often listed the London Philharmonic Orchestra, and many times, during a film, one of us would call attention to the glorious musical score. I'd never been so aware of how important a good score was for a movie. We also discovered that any movie produced by Arthur Rank would be a good one! Sir Arthur Rank, as he later was knighted.

In 1957 we saw "The Man Who Knew Too Much," and just loved it. It was an American movie but was produced and directed, of course, by an Englishman, Alfred Hitchcock, whose films always provided suspense and anticipation. James Stewart and

Doris Day (both Americans, thank goodness) were the stars. Doris sang a catchy tune that we were all whistling or humming as we left, "Que Sera Sera," which is Italian for "Whatever will be, will be." Someone said the song won an Academy Award. But my biggest thrill over the song occurred when I went home for next furlough. My four-year-old niece, Cora Rita, sang it as if it had been composed for her. My brother, Harold, insisted she was as good as — or better than — Shirley Temple! Not the least biased, of course, I agreed wholeheartedly.

Several missionaries, including myself, loved to play tennis, as did many English friends who came by after school hours so we could play. Afterwards, we'd have tea, and this became a frequent diversion. We made several friends this way, usually couples. Three, however, were brothers from Lebanon, George, Suad and Antoinne Fulogah, who operated a brokerage business in Lagos. Sometimes they'd bring fruit or baked goods or some other product they were handling, and we appreciated the gifts. But after about a year George began to display a romantic interest which was not reciprocated, so their visits slacked off and stopped completely after George and Antoine had to return to Lebanon.

In my early days in Nigeria I saw the emergence of a kind of folk opera developed, written and staged by Yoruba-speaking people. It combined bits of mime and vivid costumes with the traditional drumming, music and stories of their tribal history. The performances were primarily for Yoruba audiences, but we got to see a few of them. Several of the plays were satires on Yoruba types, such as the jealous husband, the stingy father, the reckless son, etc. Others were exposes of topical events in Nigerian politics.

— THE TWO R'S: R & R —

We were treated with civility when we attended a play, but we heard rumors that the acting company would be happier if Caucasians, especially those of the highest moral fiber (which hit us squarely between the eyes), would stay away. We wondered why.

Although these plays first appeared in the late 1930s or early 1940s, their first legitimate burst of popularity came during 1947 to 1950. Ogunde, one of the writer/producers, formed a professional company during those years, the first, to our knowledge, and paid his actors, dancers and musicians. He was also one of the first to utilize Christian teachings and materials in a couple of his story plots. We saw one of these, "The Palm Wine Drunkard," and thought it superior to earlier plays we had seen. Christian influence had actually reached into the Nigerians' entertainment.

My personal enjoyment was diminished by male singers who usually had leading roles. They seemed to delight in producing extremely high, falsetto-like notes, which to me were quite annoying and detracted from the production. I found no fault with the women. But those peculiar, high-pitched, screechy voices just didn't fit the image they were trying to portray.

This Nigerian theater, which I suppose is the correct name for it, continued to grow during the 30 years I was in Nigeria. And productions were taken to other countries, I understand, where they were either extremely popular or dismal failures. It was interesting to me, a silent spectator, to see this native art form develop and take its place in Nigerian history.

After my transfer to Jos, plays, movies, department stores and restaurants became a thing of the past, replaced by home-grown forms of R & R. With a better climate, I started and maintained my own flower garden. My roses were the most beautiful I had ever grown. I had only one year with a principal's responsibilities, then my job as a teacher in the high school provided something I'd had little of in Lagos: some very welcome leisure time. During the rainy season, it was not unusual to actually have a fire in the fireplace. The evenings were cool, sometimes down in the 40s.

Hillcrest was nearby and I got to know all of our missionary kids. I loved to entertain them, mainly by making goodies for them. We all enjoyed the school's productions of Gilbert & Sullivan operettas, Shakespeare's plays and even an ambitious staging of the popular Rodgers and Hammerstein musical "Carousel." The kids always did a splendid job.

A missionary couple, John and Louise Hill, became close friends. Louise decided that I should study the piano and painting., since she taught both. I started the piano lessons and spent half an hour daily doing finger exercises. And I bought brushes, paints and paper and began learning about strokes, mixing colors, etc. I even got a "color-by-the-number" book. Louise soon learned that desire cannot overcome a lack of talent. But I enjoyed trying.

During a furlough I learned that my brother Harold had taken up golf. He taught me the basics of the game and gave me a very basic set of clubs to take back to Nigeria. I didn't expect to play, because I hadn't seen any golf courses in Jos. But to my surprise, another missionary, Edith Nunnally, liked the game too, and we spent several hours out on rock-hard, brown fairways, knocking a ball around.

Edith had learned the game from her husband, and through her I became interested and eventually learned to love playing golf. We talked of attending the Masters Tournament in Augusta, Ga., after we retired.

THE TWO R'S: R & R

Saturday was "get-together night" for all the missionaries, and we indulged in dominoes, anagrams and, sometimes, we turned risqué and played Rook. Talk about exciting times! Well, that was it for the unattached females.

I always made certain that I got exercise by walking, working in my garden, etc., and there was one activity that took lots of exertion: climbing and exploring Gog and Magog. These two mountains near Jos were named by 19th-century British archeologists. Of course, Gog and Magog are in the Book of Revelation and are generally interpreted as being warriors of Satan who manifest themselves before the end of the world. Previous expeditions of climbers, including some missionaries, told of seeing several species of animals, including large, reddish gorilla-like creatures, up on the climbing paths. I climbed two or three times, but never saw them. Edith Nunnally told of encountering them once, which caused her some anxious moments that passed without incident.

During the climb there is a spot where one must, to complete the climb, make a short jump (18 inches to two feet) over a drop of several hundred feet. Many of the lady missionaries stopped and deliberated over the jump. Having heard this, when I reached the spot I leaped right across without hesitation, much to the dismay of others with me. When we got back to town, they made a little fuss about my rash deed. But it was frivolous and soon forgotten.

There were so many joyous and memorable moments in Nigeria that it would be impossible to recall them all. However, without our wonderful mission family and marvelous fellowship, any R & R would be quickly forgotten. Togetherness made it memorable and those times will remain a part of me for the rest of my life.

THE THREE 'R'S; 'READING, 'RITING & 'RITHMETIC

Due to colonization by Great Britain, Nigerian schools followed the British educational system and, as with all systems, it had good and bad points.

I soon learned, through experience as well as from the English themselves, that the system was different — sometimes significantly so — from one British country to another. For example, Scotland had its own system, while Wales and Ireland closely followed the English. And Canada and Australia, I was told, were different from the others.

The system enabled each country to insert subject matter about local interests, such as a country's own history, or present the same subjects with a local flavor or application. This freedom of selectivity was popular in Nigeria, as I imagine it was elsewhere.

One problem it created evolved during testing periods. For instance, tests to determine accreditation or for scholarships. These tests usually contained standard subject-matter questions and problem-solving examples that might not be part of a country's curriculum, or was a relatively small part of it. This forced us to weigh the amount of subject matter, outside the standard British testing systems, that we could permit, and to make sure sufficient standard testing matter was included, even to the point of special tutoring, if necessary.

Nigerians loved their own history and literature and it was no surprise that our students usually excelled in these areas. So many of the stories which had become myths and legends, such as "The Spider's Web," "The Rubber Man," "Thunder & Lightening," "Why the Bush Fly Calls at Dawn & Why the Flies Buzz," "Why the Sun & Moon Live in the Sky," "The Singing Drum & the Mysterious Pumpkin" and many others, had seldom been written down. But they were told over and over again, until some of the English writers, such as Kathleen Arnott, had them published, thus making them available for curriculum purposes.

Practically all study materials were British in origin and, whether a publication said The Oxford Press or some other British publishing house, one could easily tell that an author was British by the number of degrees listed after the name. This held true not only in publishing but in all business fields. An Englishman wanted each and every degree listed immediately after his name, whether that name appeared in a publication or on the front door of a business establishment. It most assuredly appeared on calling cards. We used to laugh and joke about it. But I'm certain the British found some American practices frivolous too.

Our graduates usually did very well, indeed, on their qualifying tests, and some of them had ambitions to study abroad. Several had been accepted at universities in England but none had been to the United States until the early '50s, when we obtained a scholarship for a most deserving student at Smith College in New England. We later sent students to Randolph-Macon in Virginia, Centre College in Kentucky (was I proud of my own home state!) and Swarthmore in Pennsylvania, all private schools with excellent academic credentials. This led to a succession of acceptances at public schools, starting with University of Michigan in Ann Arbor.

Preparing our girls for the local language, dress, customs and academic structure was difficult, but the hardest things to impart were of a social nature. For instance, how would you prepare an 18-

year-old who had been taught and was striving to obey Christian principles, about racial discrimination? She had been taught by Americans to believe that God loves everyone, and now those Americans were trying to prepare her for the clash of truth versus fiction she would experience when she went to America.

There was no way to disguise it. But reviewing the history of the United States, with its days of slavery followed by abolition, seemed to provide the needed insight. Most could understand how, decades later, some of the old despitefulness could remain.

The greatest challenge the girls had to overcome was the frigid climate in the United States and, for that matter, England. They had seen pictures of snow and had read about it in books, but even returning students could not successfully impart the impact it made on them.

One day I had an idea. I took two girls to my kitchen and opened the door of the fridge so they could touch the white, shiny frost on the ice compartment.

"Oh-h-h-h!" they screamed, quickly pulling their fingers away, "that's terrible!"

'Well," I said, "when you encounter ice, that's exactly how it will feel. But snow usually falls down from the sky in soft, white, fluffy petals and you can catch them and it won't hurt. But once it covers the ground, then its a lot like the frost you just touched."

They looked at each other in astonishment. From that day on, we used the fridge to illustrate how a snowy and icy climate would feel.

Although local history was part of the curriculum, British history was a requirement. The British version of events sometimes had a different slant, so our missionary teachers provided additional information.

THE THREE 'R'S

A good example is the Rebellion of the American Colonies, as the British history books stated it. In effect, the American colonies were a violent, rebellious people who, despite all that King George tried to do for them, were backwoods ingrates, unlike their neighboring colony, Canada, to the north. The Revolutionary War, as the American history books call it, was covered in only a brief paragraph or two. The same held true for the War of 1812, except in this war, considerable was made over the British capturing New York City and burning our capitol, Washington D. C. Admiral Perry's victories over the British on the Great Lakes and the Battle of New Orleans, in which the British suffered a crushing defeat, were not mentioned.

I always laugh when I remember Polly Van Lear, who was teaching English history. She left our early-morning huddle for her class, telling us, "Well, I've got to go and acquaint my class with the nuances of the REBELLION OF THE COLONIES this morning." Then she paused, looked back and added with a wink, "I told them yesterday to read it well because today I was going to tell them HOW IT REALLY HAPPENED!" I wish I had been there to hear her, as well as the discussion that surely followed.

Some of the most important days of the year were Sports Days. We usually had three or four a year. Most of the girls loved to run, jump and perform other feats of dexterity, and some were extremely adept. We prepared for each Sports Day and did it as professionally and with as much fanfare as we could. I recall one girl who could jump as high as she was tall. I believe the girls liked the relays best, and this pleased the teachers because success depended so much on the TEAM instead of the individual.

Occasionally we invited some of our male missionaries over to serve as officials and do some coaching. I don't know which group liked this better, the men or the girls. During one Sports Day, Marjorie McCullough, one of our fine teachers, and I decided to provide a special treat for the girls by racing each other! I don't recall how or why the race began or the distance we ran, but we were side by side all the way. Students were jumping up and down on the sidelines, screaming encouragement to both of us. I believe

Miss Anita Roper and Cora Ney.

we surprised ourselves and exerted far more energy than we thought we possessed.

We crossed the finish line dead even. Marjorie, however, borrowed a horse-racing phrase and declared that I had won the race "by a nose." If true, it was only so because my nose must be a fraction of an inch longer than hers, and that was no compliment!

As I recall those school days I realize how fortunate I was to have such wonderfully qualified teachers, both missionaries and, later, Nigerians, without whom our school would never have grown and succeeded as it did. I keep thinking that I never gave anywhere near enough expressions of appreciation to them nor thanks to God for this.

Anita Roper, from Georgia, was there even longer than I, because she remained after I was transferred north. I think we made an incomparable team, and I appreciated and thanked the Lord for her so often.

At the risk of overlooking someone, I also must mention invaluable help from others such as Mary Jane Whorton from Alabama, Mary Frank Kirkpatrick, Dale Moore, Maxine Lockhart and Alma Rohn, all from Texas, Marjorie McCullough from Louisiana and Marie Van Lear from Virginia. No school ever possessed more dedicated and capable teachers and educators.

A DESPERATE JOURNEY

After my transfer to Jos, armed uprisings, coups and rumors of both erupted. The country was divided into four major states and its civilian government had little power. Then the Army assumed control in 1966-67 and restructured Nigeria into 12 states.

All this upheaval did not surprise us. In our efforts to reach as many of the different peoples as possible, we became acutely aware of their vast differences, mistrusts and possessiveness.

One of the largest and oldest groups were the Fulani. At one time they resided — and still do to a great degree — in the northern part of the country. Through the years they interbred with Arabs, not surprising, as they were near the Arab countries north of Nigeria. They bore the brunt of the annual Harmattan there, a fierce wind that came screaming out of the Sahara Desert during the dry season, carrying its sand all the way down to Nigeria.

The major religion of the Fulani was Muslim, although, through our efforts — limited because the Fulani were most reluctant to have anything to do with our missionaries — we had made a small dent in their armor. The potential, as well as the future, looked quite promising. The Fulani had scattered small portions of their people throughout Nigeria, but their stronghold remained in the north where their basic trades were herding and agricultural. Many decades ago the Fulani warred with the Hausa people and conquered them. Now, curiously, the Hausa language was second only to the Yoruba language in Nigeria.

Intermarriage had created a unique people, taller than other Nigerians, with a range of Negroid and non-Negroid physical traits that included straight noses (as opposed to flat noses), relatively thin lips (as opposed to thick lips), straight hair and thin bone structure. Interbreeding with Arabs and Caucasoid people (believed to be Berbers) is the general explanation for this divergence.

At the time of the Biafran Civil War in 1966-67, we had two Fulani students in our boys' high school in Jos. When tales of atrocities committed in the war — many against the Fulani peoples — reached the school these two boys pleaded desperately to be permitted to return home. Their fear for their families' welfare was heartbreaking and understandable. However, our men knew that they'd never have a chance, on their own, to get through the warring factions to their people.

So two of our preachers took matters into their own hands. I won't give their names, for obvious reasons, but they both had families who agreed for them to act. They took one of our larger vehicles and lowered the floor of the back seat about 8 to10 inches.. Then they built a new floor 8 to10 inches higher than the original one. This provided enough space for the boys to lie down, hidden from view.

The plan was for them to sit in the back seat until the men in front signaled them. Then they would lie down on the lower floor and be covered by the other floor. A floor rug would be laid over the upper floor, and some boxes of auto tools placed on the rug.

The two men said an impassioned good-bye to their wives and children, knowing they might never see them again. We all watched as they drove out of sight. We knew they would encounter the Fulani's enemies on the way, probably at the point where two states joined territories. And there could be more than one perilous encounter on this journey.

The days lingered by, sunset to sunset, with our prayers and longing increasing each day. Never had I seen such brave women as those two wives. I gained an even greater insight into the uncontrollable longing that many American wives experienced during World War II when their husbands were away.

News of the Civil War was intermittent and incomplete. Our lives and school functions continued without interference. For this we were grateful. Only a handful of us actually knew the purpose of this journey, for the men felt that the fewer who knew about their mission, the safer it would be. Weeks passed and we heard nothing. But what they were doing was compassionate, and we felt that, with God's guidance, they would succeed.

But the days continued on and on with no news. Faith was still strong, but longing was even stronger.

One evening, as we sat outside our houses, someone saw a tiny speck of light out in the countryside. She stood up and pointed in that direction.

"Did you see that?" she asked. "It was just about there."

No one else had. But we waited, standing to get a better view through the oncoming darkness.

Then suddenly we could all see it, moving along jerkily, bouncing up and down just like an automobile traveling over rough terrain. Still, we were cautious. It could be an Army auto bringing news of their capture. Or they might be coming to arrest some of us for helping. We waited with stifled breath.

Soon we could see the outline of the vehicle, and it was OURS! Their arrival was filled with hugs, kisses, tears, slaps on the back and silent prayers of thankfulness. After a hearty meal, with all gathered around the table, the two heroes told of their adventure.

They had no trouble crossing the enemy line, they said. The officers in charge stopped them, asked for identification and walked around the vehicle. Then they were told to "Proceed."

"We're missionaries," they responded to questioning, "and we have people up ahead we must see. Provided, of course, it is all right with you. No, we have no firearms or ammunition; nor do we have documents or messages to deliver." Nothing was mentioned about smuggling or human cargo, so their consciences were clear.

Coming back was a different story, however. They were stopped and questioned at length and the vehicle got a thorough search. The men didn't worry, because they had removed the upper floor in the back. The soldiers looked at the sub-floor, but if they noticed it was lower than usual, they made no objection. We all felt the Lord had made certain that if a search was to be made, it would be done when the boys weren't in the vehicle.

The men had carried sufficient petrol (gas, to Americans) for the return trip, so they didn't risk driving into the boys' villages, but let them out a mile or so away. The boys felt that if their villages were occupied by the enemy, they could reach their families easier if they were alone.

We all slept better that night than we had in weeks, and the prayers of thanksgiving that were said when they arrived turned into very vocal ones before we "hit the sack"!

I knew of episodes similar to this one which commanded heroic efforts and deeds. Only through the ever-present, watchful eyes of God did they always succeed, proving what I have always felt — our Father does, indeed, watch over His own.

FURLOUGH

Furlough. What a magical word it was. I literally lived for my furloughs. My longing for family and friends while I was in Africa was beyond belief. My first African Christmas was in 1947, my first Christmas, ever, away from home and, oh, how homesick I was! John and Nina Mills, a couple from Texas, came out about the same time and were having just as difficult a time. But, together, we helped each other through the holiday, forming a bond that will last forever. At the time, John was a missionary evangelist in Lagos, but he moved on to other positions, eventually assuming responsibility for all of our West African operations.

That first Christmas I realized why the song "White Christmas" had gained instant popularity with our World War II servicemen, particularly those serving in the hot and humid South Pacific climate, so similar to ours in Lagos. During my subsequent tours, the first Christmas back in Africa was always tougher because memories of the previous one spent at home were still so strong. Conversely, the easiest Christmas was the last one prior to leaving on furlough because I knew I would spend the next one at home.

When I went home for my first furlough in 1950, I had actually forgotten how even my closest relatives and friends looked. Oh, I could remember them and I had pictures, of course, but the details of their faces and their expressions were not clear. But at first sight of them it all returned.

My first three furloughs were spent with my sister, Margaret, her husband Roy and their family in their Louisville home. Their eldest child, Bucky was about one-and-a-half-years old, and during my stay, their second, Denny, was born. The love I'd showered on my nephew before I went to Africa was quickly transferred to Bucky, and it broke my heart to leave him when my furlough ended. Both he and Denny, along with the other four who arrived in the years ahead, were like my very own and I knew they felt the same towards me. Although I didn't get to see them as frequently nor for as long a time as my other nieces and nephews, my brother Robert and his wife, Elizabeth, were blessed with two wonderful daughters, Sandra and Suzanne. I counted them as my blessings, too.

I spent an enormous amount of time traveling to different churches and towns speaking about my work in Nigeria, showing slides I'd taken, curios I'd brought back and dressing lady volunteers

Christmas with Cora Ney's sister's family.

in the Nigerian clothes I had brought home. I enjoyed this immensely because, in addition to the fun I had, I learned about young girls in my audiences who later became missionaries. What better way could I have spent my time?

I also began preliminary classes toward a master's degree in education at the University of Louisville. The campus was only a few miles from my sister's home.

In March, 1951, the weekend before I went back to Lagos, I saw my very first basketball game on television. Now, being a Kentuckian, for me the game was inborn. And I vividly recall, although I was only four or five at the time, when my first cousin, Sam Ridgeway, from Shepherdsville, was captain of the University of Kentucky's basketball team, the Wildcats. That was around 1920. He was a local hero and, to me, he always seemed eight feet tall, he was so big! Bucky played at UK in the 1960s, and his father, Roy, had a cousin who was an All-American there in the 1940s.

We were joined that evening by two dear friends, Pete and Marge Trunnell, to watch the game on TV. Today, some people think that girls' basketball is new. But Marge had been a very good player on our Shepherdsville High School girls' team in the 1920s, so we all had a keen interest in the game. And what a game it was! UK versus Illinois in the NCAA Final Four. They put on quite a show. We were out of our chairs, on our feet or down on the floor, all the time cheering like mad. And when Kentucky won the game with a last-minute basket, we celebrated as if we were there. What a way to spend my last weekend of furlough!

That night, I decided to take a basketball goal back to Nigeria with me. So Roy bought one, crated it for overseas shipment and I did. At Reagan, our carpenter made the backboard and mounted it on a pole and our girls took to the game like fish to water, playing with a soccer ball. I had changed the school colors from purple and white to blue and white, so our games took on a real Kentucky flavor. Years later, while I was in Jos watching our MK high-school team play the Nigerian high-school team, someone pointed me out as the one who introduced the American game of basketball to West Africa. There had been teams elsewhere on the continent, in Egypt and Ethiopia, but there was no record of any West African countries playing the sport before I brought that goal back with me in 1951.

During my first furlough I received a cablegram from London. It was from an Englishman I had met in Nigeria. He was back in England on "holiday," as the British put it, and he was, of all things, proposing marriage to me. I crumpled up the cablegram and threw it in the waste basket in disgust, muttering a few words about it to Margaret. She retrieved it, saying, "Now, let's not make up our minds so quickly."

"Don't give it a second thought. My mind is made up," I retorted. "It would take more than that Englishman to make me give up my freedom! Of all the egotistical nerve!"

She was amazed, for, you see, all my family feared I would be an old maid. As far as I was concerned, I already was, and hadn't anticipated anything that would change the situation. After Margaret questioned me about the man, she understood my disgust.

He had dated one of our missionaries and, about a year before I went out, she resigned and married him. He was the British representative for a large company and they lived in a very nice home with servants. However, the other missionaries told me she had changed after the marriage. She seemed uncertain of herself and terribly unhappy. During my furlough I heard that she had committed suicide.

Now here he was proposing to me so soon afterwards — I had only been around him twice — and by cablegram!

Margaret understood my feelings about him and agreed with me. But my brother Harold heard about the proposal from Margaret and made a special trip from Shepherdsville to Louisville to talk to me.

"Now, Toady," he began, "let's talk about this thing." He always called me Toady, the name many of us called our favorite aunt, Cora Roby, for whom I was named.

"Harold," I responded calmly, "as far as I'm concerned there's absolutely nothing to talk about. I hardly know the man and what I do know about him, I don't care for."

Serene quiet reigned for a minute or two.

"You know something, Toady?" His voice was firmer but conciliatory. "One of your hang-ups, and I've come close to saying this to you several times, is that you expect entirely too much in a man! Do you understand what I'm saying?"

I smiled and looked at him as if I thought he was crazy.

"You expect to find the perfect man . . . and, frankly, he doesn't exist." Harold paused for a moment, then continued. "You've established this fabricated image of the man you would marry, and anything less than this fantasy image just won't do."

"Harold," I said softly, taking his hand and looking straight into his eyes, "if my ideal for the man I would accept for a husband doesn't exist, then I'm never going to marry."

That ended our conversation.

During that first furlough Aunt Cora asked to see me and I went to her home in Shepherdsville. She always treated me like royalty. No one in our family was more loved and respected than Aunt Toady. She was as close to being the matriarch of our family as you could get.

"Honey Child," she began, "I've been thinking about something ever since you went away and it has bothered me constantly."

"What on earth is it, Aunt Toady?" I asked, fearing that something horrible had happened.

"I just cannot recall, from my early childhood, ever making a public profession of my faith in Jesus Christ as my Savior," she said. "Oh, I thought I had been a Christian all of my 66 years but," she paused and looked at me searchingly, "but I can't be, can I, unless I've made public profession of my belief?"

What I experienced during the next hour will remain with me all my life. I was responsible for my own beloved Aunt Toady questioning her faith and its validity. She wanted to make that profession and then follow through with baptism — she was not a true Christian until she had done so. Two weeks later she had completed both and the satisfaction I felt, seeing her go through this test of faith and courage, was one of the greatest experiences of my life. Bruce Hartsell, pastor of Shepherdsville Baptist Church at that time, performed the services and he and his wife, Dorothy, who taught piano at the Southern Seminary Music School for 18 years, became close friends with our family, especially Margaret's family and me. We enjoyed many wonderful times together over the years.

★ ★ ★

"For goodness sake," I exclaimed as I stepped from my plane onto the exit ramp. "Where did you all come from? Who is here?"

Arriving home for my second furlough in May, 1954, I found some three dozen kinfolk waiting to greet me. What a splendid surprise!

Then I realized it was May 10, MY BIRTHDAY, and this explained it all. It was a beautiful present, immensely appreciated.

On May 18, Margaret gave birth to a cute little girl and named her Cora Rita, after me. This pleased me far more than anyone ever knew. Four generations of Coras now made up our lineage. The latest one grew up to be a living doll and I spoiled her terribly, taking her with me just about everywhere I went.

Also, during this furlough, I made a huge dent in my university credits toward my master's degree.

During my third furlough, in 1959, I obtained my master's degree in education.

Bill and Audrey Cowley, who had arrived in Nigeria in 1955, were studying at Southern Seminary during their first furlough. Bill was principal at the boys' mission school, Baptist Academy, just a few miles from Reagan Memorial. While they were at the seminary they visited me and got to know Margaret and her family.

The deadline for my graduate-school thesis was rapidly approaching when I turned it over to a highly-recommended lady to be typed. I agreed to a higher per-page fee than usual and authorized her to correct any typographical or grammatical errors she might find. I was going to the annual Southern Baptist Convention and would get back only a day or two before the thesis was due. I felt secure about this because the typist was recommended to me by the university staff. I even told her to turn it in when she finished.

While I was at the convention Margaret called me, because she had heard from the university that my thesis had been turned in but was totally unacceptable. Apparently the lady in whom I had placed such trust had done an atrocious job of typing and had even inserted some of her own irrelevant comments. I was devastated. I knew there would not be time to redo it. I would have to wait until my next furlough to complete my degree.

Audrey and Bill heard about my dilemma and volunteered to take on the huge re-typing task. They rented identical typewriters so both could work at the same time and the type would be identical. God bless them, they finished it just in time for me to meet the deadline. There are some things in life for which there are simply no words or ways to say "thank you" sufficiently — and this was certainly one of them.

My sister-in-law, Kay, Harold's wife, had been working toward the identical goal and we got our degrees at the same graduation ceremony. But a master's degree was not to be my stopping place. I wanted a doctorate and I wanted it badly and I wanted it from the University of Kentucky. My brother Robert had received his engineering degree from UK. If I could get a doctorate there I would have degrees from four different state schools: Western Kentucky University, Southern Seminary Carver School of Missions, the University of Louisville and the University of Kentucky. So I hoped and prayed my final degree would be from UK.

During my fifth furlough, Margaret and her family were living in Michigan and I stayed with Harold and Kay in Louisville. But I spent almost as much time in Michigan. I couldn't stay away from the children for too long and of course I had to spend Christmas with them. Their fifth child, Van, was born while I was home, the first out-of-state birth.

Harold's regular golf foursome included a Shepherdsville attorney, "Jiggs" Buckman, who was the district's elected representative to Frankfort. He kept bugging Harold to get me to address an opening session of the State Legislature. Speaking to a group of politicians was the last thing I wanted to do. But one day in Shepherdsville Jiggs saw me, approached and made the request in such a plaintive way that, in a weak moment, I agreed. The time was set for opening day of the fall session.

I chided myself for giving in. I was scheduled to speak "for about five minutes," and I hadn't the slightest idea what to say. Thinking about it, I realized the Legislative Chaplain would give the opening invocation, so what was left for me to say?

After considerable thought, I decided to speak on living life on a day-to-day basis and doing our best each day, basing my comments on Psalm 118:34 (THIS IS THE DAY THE LORD HATH MADE; WE WILL REJOICE AND BE GLAD IN IT).

Their response was most gratifying. Many of the legislators came forward at recess, when I was leaving, to introduce themselves and tell me how appropriate my talk had been and how much they appreciated it. One such gentleman, Gene Snyder, had just been elected to the U. S. Congress in Washington, D. C. When he learned that I had a brother, Robert, a short distance away in Portsmouth, Va., he insisted I visit him when I visited Robert again. Since I had no plans for another visit during this furlough, I dismissed any thought of taking him up on his invitation. But during the next three years in Nigeria, I continually received reminders from both Harold and Jiggs, that Congressman Snyder was counting on my visiting him with my brother during my next furlough.

I had never visited our nation's capitol and it was one thing I always planned to do. I believe, as Americans living in the greatest

Congressman Gene Snyder and Miss Hardy in Washington D.C.

nation on earth, we should all make every effort to see our capitol. So I wrote to Robert and when I returned to the States in 1966, I arranged to come through Portsmouth first. In fact, Robert, his wife and their two lovely daughters met me in Richmond, Va., and we drove to Washington from there. Congressman Snyder was even better than his word. He devoted almost an entire day to showing us the sights. He even had a photographer take a photograph of the two of us sitting at his office desk.

Every time I go to Louisville I am reminded of this experience for, you see, the outer highway loop around the city, Interstate 465 — the GENE SNYDER EXPRESSWAY — is named after this gentleman.

My sister passed away in September, 1975.

Five days before her death, Roy cabled me that she was failing fast. She and I were always very, very close, and if there was any possible way, I wanted to be there. But could I arrive in time? My missionary family in Jos, as well as in Lagos, worked miracle after miracle to get me ready, obtain my ticket, handle my routing through the main airport at Lagos, which was a traveling nightmare. I know the Lord was watching over me, because everything went as planned. I arrived home early on a Friday afternoon. Roy and Cora Rita were waiting at the International Terminal to meet me. Getting through customs usually took a long time, but I went through this time with a minimum of delays.

Roy and Cora Rita got me to the hospital by mid-afternoon and, seeing Margaret's condition, I wanted to burst out crying. But the gleam that appeared in her eyes when she saw me told me everything was fine. I was there with her. The cancer, which had taken her left breast nine months earlier, had expanded into every part of her body.

We laughed and talked about many things and she showed, despite periodic spasms of pain, great courage and stamina — all she had left to give. Before I left for the night, we prayed, and I promised her I would be back very early the next morning.

How good the Lord is to us, more than we stop to realize, I truly believe. Next morning I arrived at the hospital to learn that she had fallen into a coma during the night. She knew no one from that point on and the next afternoon she was gone. How grateful I was for that last opportunity to see and talk with her.

And I'll never forget how bravely the three youngest children, Guy, Van and Tony, took the news as Roy gathered them around him and told them.

How I felt for those children, now motherless, and how I hated returning to Nigeria and leaving them. I cried all the way back. I kept a close correspondence going between us until my work and time, to a degree, lessened the pain. Although we should never question the Lord, I kept wondering why he hadn't taken me instead of Margaret. My work was practically finished. I had made my major contributions to the work there in Nigeria, while she still had a six-year-old to rear. Of course, we never question — we accept.

My final furlough came in late 1976, and though I stayed again with Harold and Kay in Kentucky, my heart was with Margaret's children. Cora Rita had married and Roy was performing the roles of father and mother very well, indeed. As usual, my time was spent traveling and speaking to churches everywhere. But I did squeeze in time to visit the children.

During previous visits I had made several talks to churches in the suburban Chicago area where Roy and the children lived, so it was not unusual that they received several calls for me to speak during the December Lottie Moon Christmas Mission Offerings. We worked out the dates by phone, and to avoid conflicts I decided to spend the entire month of December with them, the delightful prospect of Christmas foremost in my mind. I'd never missed a Christmas with them each furlough home and I wasn't going to start now. Bucky, Denny and Cora Rita would also be there with their spouses.

Its odd that I received proposals on both my first and my last furloughs. But their origins were decidedly different.

The morning after I arrived the children left for school and Roy and I sat in the kitchen. I was talking about this being my final furlough. He listened intently and then asked what I planned to do during retirement. I said I hoped to share an apartment with, perhaps, another retired missionary and obtain some kind of position with a church in Louisville, where I planned to live.

"You know, don't you," Roy said, "that Margaret and I had always planned on your living with us?"

I replied that I knew we had all been close but I was not aware of any such plans.

He then made a very nice proposal of marriage. "I know how you feel about the children, and they about you," he emphasized.

"I've always regarded you as my brother, a very dear brother," I interrupted, taken aback. "I'm just as fond of you as I am my biological brothers, Robert and Harold . . . but . . . marriage . . . ." I stopped short.

There was a brief pause.

"Surely there are other women that you would want as your wife, aren't there?" I asked.

He laughed and replied, "Oh yes, there are several. Cora Ney, you wouldn't believe how a widower draws sugar!" We both laughed, for I could easily imagine how a nice-looking man like Roy, complete with a home and means and all, would be attractive to women.

"Why," he continued, "I've heard from ladies that I haven't even seen in over 20 years! Word gets around, and friends, especially women, just can't stand for a man to be unattached."

'Well," I said, "you should explore all the possibilities before you decide to remarry."

"Indeed I have," he responded, "and there is not a woman alive

I would give a second look. Except you." Then he came over to me and asked, "Will you give it consideration?"

I was completely overwhelmed by his sincerity.

"I'll need some time to think it over,' I said, and my concentrated, deep-soul deliberations began. I wasn't the same the rest of the day and I slept very little that night. Next morning I had reached a decision and as soon as the children left, I told Roy. "I've decided to accept your proposal. I've given 30 years to the children of Africa. Now I think its appropriate for me to give some time to my sister's children."

He gave me a kiss and said, "Thank you. I'll do everything I can to make you happy." And he did.

The following weeks were a blur of activity with my speaking engagements, Christmas shopping, wrapping presents, putting up the tree and decorations and other holiday activities. But Roy took time to escort me to a jeweler's, where I picked out my ring. This was exciting, for I had accepted the idea that I would never receive one. We told the children Christmas morning, after all the presents were opened. They were beside themselves with joy and good wishes.

Now I don't have to worry about Tony any longer," Cora Rita cried out. "He's going to have the best mother possible."

The family was equally pleased. Even dear Aunt Cora, whose health was failing rapidly, from her hospital bed said "Now, I approve wholeheartedly."

Part of our agreement was that I'd go back to Nigeria until July to complete 30 years of service. But when I returned with news of my impending marriage, my mission family would have none of that "July business".

"You're finishing up here as quickly as you can," they all insisted, "and getting yourself back for that wedding!"

My possessions disappeared quickly. What I didn't need I sold or gave away. (Roy had much more at home than I had in the field.) What I wanted to keep was soon packed and crated for shipment.

The boys at school gave me plaques, poems, good wishes and a wonderful book entitled "Mother." It touched me very much.

Gene Leftwich was the informal toastmaster at my farewell dinner. After everyone else had their say, he closed with a few reminiscences and then listed some of my accomplishments in almost 30 years of service. He ended with what we all thought a most appropriate comment: "But she saved the very best till last!"

I was in Nigeria only a bit over three weeks, but I missed Roy terribly. Some may have thought ours a marriage of convenience, but during that time of separation it became real. I simply couldn't wait to get back to him and — MY — family.

I transferred planes in Amsterdam and called Roy from the airport there to let him know I wasn't staying until July and tell him how much I had missed him.

My closing sentence was, "I'll never put an ocean between us again!"

And I never did.

BRIEF BIOGRAPHY

Cora Ney Hardy Jones was born in rural Bullitt County, Ky., on May 10, 1915. At age 10, with both her father and mother working to make ends meet, she assumed all household duties including cooking, cleaning and sewing, as well as caring for her younger brother and sister.

School was her favorite time and she decided at a very early age to become a teacher.

She graduated from Shepherdsville High School at mid-term her senior year and hastened off to Western Kentucky State Teachers' College, now Western Kentucky University in Bowling Green, where she worked at various office and cafeteria jobs to help earn a Bachelor's Degree in Education, which she obtained with high marks in only three-and-a-half years. Succeeding years found her teaching elementary school in rural Bullitt and Jefferson counties, including schools of the one-room variety with a pot-bellied stove, where she was also a nurse, cook, surrogate mother and anything else required.

In 1942, feeling a duty to do something for her country's war effort, she left teaching temporarily to work in the personnel office of a large munitions manufacturing company in Charlestown, Ind. She made such a favorable impression that, immediately upon war's end, the company, DuPont, wanted to transfer her to their main offices in Delaware. Although tempted, she did not want to give up teaching or leave her family and her beloved Kentucky.

However, something had been gnawing at her insides since her teen-age years. She experienced a calling that she kept sweeping aside and tried to ignore. This inner struggle became so fierce she found herself unable to sing the hymn, "Wherever He Leads I'll Go," whenever it was sung in church.

Before returning to teaching she decided to end this conflict once and for all. She wrote to her church's Foreign Mission Board inquiring if there would be a place for her in God's service. She hoped, prayed and believed that the response would be "no." Then she'd have freed herself to brush off this inner annoyance and return to teaching. But the reply stated, "PREPARE. WE NEED YOU!" This was now clear enough. She took the funds she'd saved from her wartime defense-plant job and entered the Carver School of Missions of the Southern Baptist Seminary in Louisville. After obtaining a Master of Religious Education degree two years later, she was assigned to service as a schoolteacher in Nigeria, West Africa.

After a tearful farewell to family, friends, Kentucky and the good old USA, she left for Africa. Miss Hardy soon learned that she was not just going to be a teacher but also the principal of a girls' school in Lagos, Nigeria, the capitol city.

A meeting two weeks later resulted in her being charged with the responsibility of expanding the school to high school level. With the training of Africans who could, eventually, succeed them as educators, along with a few new missionaries from the States, not to mention 16- to 18-hour days, Miss Hardy and her staff successfully accomplished this challenge and obtained school accreditation in the tough British Educational System. Nigeria was a British colony at the time.

After Nigeria gained it's independence in 1960 and sufficient graduates were qualified to assume leadership in the school, Miss

— BIOGRAPHY —

Hardy was relieved of her duties there and sent to the northern part of Nigeria to teach in a boys' high school. Although this was not as prestigious a position, the climate was much more suitable.

Each of her furloughs (every four years) was spent with her sister and brother-in-law, Margaret and Roy Jones, and their growing family. Miss Hardy spoke to churches and other groups while on furlough. And she always had time for the Jones' six children, three of whom were born while she was home. They all loved "Auntie," as they called her. Every fourth Christmas at home became her most anticipated event.

In 1975, Margaret died of cancer, leaving three of the younger children at home with no mother. Receiving word of her sister's impending death, Miss Hardy arrived just in time for a final reunion before Margaret expired. Two years later she was home again for her final furlough before retirement. Roy asked about her retirement plans. She had nothing definite. He proposed marriage, reminding her that he and Margaret had always planned on her living with them when she retired. Completely surprised, she "thought it over" very carefully before accepting, commenting that she had "given 30 years to the children of Africa and now it is appropriate I give some time to my sister's children."

They were married in 1977 and lived many years in Minneapolis, Minn. When Roy retired, and with all the children now grown and gone, the couple returned to their beloved Kentucky to live. It was a lifetime dream to go home. They looked forward to a relaxed lifestyle, but it wasn't to be. First, an automobile accident curtailed their plans. Then she learned she was losing her eyesight, and afterwards, a series of health problems developed.

Despite these setbacks, she thoroughly enjoyed the return to her native state. Her happiest times were spent taking her grandchildren around the state showing them its beauty and visiting landmarks and historic sites such as the Kentucky Horse Park, Daniel Boone National Forest, My Old Kentucky Home, Fort Harrod and Mammoth Cave. And she continued visiting churches, talking to young and old alike about her years in Foreign Mission service which remained so close to her heart.

Urged by Roy and some friends, she embarked on one final accomplishment which she had wanted all her life — a doctoral degree from the University of Kentucky. Because her eyesight was less than 10%, she was permitted to use a tape recorder in class, and Roy assisted her with the reading and writing assignments. She was able to achieve almost half of her required credits with a perfect 4.0 grade point-average. It was during one of her UK classes that a professor noticed a change in her ability to communicate and comprehend and brought it to Roy's attention. The diagnosis was Alzheimer's disease and this slowly debilitating malady led to her death in 1997. Roy was at her side during her final minutes.

Truly, hers was a life well-lived, and in this, her own recollections of some of her experiences in serving the Lord, she recounts several of the serious as well as humorous happenings during her African tenure of 30 years. It makes for entertaining reading as her words unfold those wonderful adventures.